New Directions for
Teaching and Learning

Marilla D. Svinicki
EDITOR-IN-CHIEF

R. Eugene Rice
CONSULTING EDITOR

Building
Faculty Learning
Communities

Milton D. Cox
Laurie Richlin
EDITORS

Number 97 • Spring 2004
Jossey-Bass
San Francisco

BUILDING FACULTY LEARNING COMMUNITIES
Milton D. Cox, Laurie Richlin (eds.)
New Directions for Teaching and Learning, no. 97
Marilla D. Svinicki, Editor-in-Chief
R. Eugene Rice, Consulting Editor

Microfilm copies of issues and articles are available in 16mm and 35mm, as well as microfiche in 105mm, through University Microfilms Inc., 300 North Zeeb Road, Ann Arbor, Michigan 48106-1346.

NEW DIRECTIONS FOR TEACHING AND LEARNING (ISSN 0271-0633, electronic ISSN 1536-0768) is part of The Jossey-Bass Higher and Adult Education Series and is published quarterly by Wiley Subscription Services, Inc., A Wiley Company, at Jossey-Bass, 989 Market Street, San Francisco, California 94103-1741. Periodicals postage paid at San Francisco, California, and at additional mailing offices. POSTMASTER: Send address changes to New Directions for Teaching and Learning, Jossey-Bass, 989 Market Street, San Francisco, California 94103-1741.

New Directions for Teaching and Learning is indexed in College Student Personnel Abstracts, Contents Pages in Education, and Current Index to Journals in Education (ERIC).

SUBSCRIPTIONS cost $80 for individuals and $160 for institutions, agencies, and libraries. Prices subject to change. See order form at end of book.

EDITORIAL CORRESPONDENCE should be sent to the editor-in-chief, Marilla D. Svinicki, The Center for Teaching Effectiveness, University of Texas at Austin, Main Building 2200, Austin, TX 78712-1111.

www.josseybass.com

CONTENTS

FROM THE SERIES EDITOR

About This Publication. Since 1980, *New Directions for Teaching and Learning (NDTL)* has brought a unique blend of theory, research, and practice to leaders in postsecondary education. *NDTL* sourcebooks strive not only for solid substance but also for timeliness, compactness, and accessibility.

The series has four goals: to inform readers about current and future directions in teaching and learning in postsecondary education, to illuminate the context that shapes these new directions, to illustrate these new directions through examples from real settings, and to propose ways in which these new directions can be incorporated into still other settings.

This publication reflects the view that teaching deserves respect as a high form of scholarship. We believe that significant scholarship is conducted not only by researchers who report results of empirical investigations but also by practitioners who share disciplined reflections about teaching. Contributors to *NDTL* approach questions of teaching and learning as seriously as they approach substantive questions in their own disciplines, and they deal not only with pedagogical issues but also with the intellectual and social context in which these issues arise. Authors deal on the one hand with theory and research and on the other with practice, and they translate from research and theory to practice and back again.

About This Volume. The rise of learning communities among faculty members at institutions of all sizes and types seems to harken back to the original purpose of a university as a place where great minds came together. These days new faculty often complain that this expected ideal is not the reality. Experienced faculty speak of being isolated in their classrooms and missing the give and take of graduate life. The faculty learning communities movement can be a solution for these and many other problems of today's diverse institutions. This issue provides both the theory and practice needed for bringing these communities to life on your campus.

Marilla D. Svinicki
Editor-in-Chief

MARILLA D. SVINICKI *is director of the Center for Teaching Effectiveness at the University of Texas at Austin.*

EDITORS' NOTES

Since early in the last century, faculty members have lamented about the isolated nature of higher education and the effects of isolation on learning, classrooms, departments, curricula, and institutions (Waller, 1932; Dewey, 1933; Meiklejohn, 1932). In the last fifteen years, the search for community has intensified (Angelo, 2000; Boyer, 1990; Gabelnick, MacGregor, Matthews, and Smith, 1990; McDonald, 2002; Palmer, 2002; Shulman, 1993).

In 1974, the Lilly Endowment provided funding for a junior faculty teaching development structure, which was modified in 1979 by Miami University to emphasize community and the scholarship of teaching. The adapted model opened a way to establish meaningful community across disciplines, curricula, and institutions. Expanded and tested for twenty-four years at Miami University and directly adapted in the last four years by over sixty other institutions, the Miami University model for faculty learning communities (FLCs) is providing a broad perspective on the search for community and a promising solution to the problems caused by the isolation that still permeates academe.

At this point in FLC history, the focus is on the practitioners who have solved the issues of initiating, managing, and facilitating FLCs. The next focus will be on the outcomes from assessment of participants in these FLCs, which should be available in the next five years. The FLC approach offers great potential for addressing institutional interests by connecting colleagues across disciplines and departments, and the FLC movement is ready to expand from the colleges and universities of early practitioners to institutions that are willing to explore and initiate FLC programs. These early practitioners, the authors of the chapters in this book, explain how and why.

In Chapter One, Cox defines a faculty learning community, places the concept in the context of related efforts, and provides goals, outcomes, needs met, community-building requirements, and components of an FLC and an FLC program. Richlin and Essington report the results of a national survey of FLCs in Chapter Two, providing an overview of the many cohort-based and topic-based types of FLCs, their relationship to institutional classification and FLC budgets, kinds and frequency of meetings, and other FLC components. In Chapter Three, Shulman, Cox, and Richlin focus on the key institutional factors that enable or hinder the development of an FLC program. The degree to which an institution can become a learning organization—its capacity for making connections—can influence the chances of successful FLC program implementation and is later strengthened by the presence of an FLC program.

In the FLC dissemination project supported in part by the Fund for the Improvement of Post-Secondary Education (FIPSE), one of the most important lessons learned has been the importance of identifying and training those who will facilitate an FLC. Sandell, Wigley, and Kovalchick report in Chapter Four on the summer institute for new FLC developers and the innovative approaches that they developed at their own universities. In Chapter Five, Petrone and Ortquist-Ahrens address questions about effective facilitation processes and the pitfalls to avoid in this key role. The facilitator entrusted with the support of FLC colleagues often is assuming this task for the first time.

In Chapter Six, Hansen, Kalish, Hall, Gynn, Holly, and Madigan describe the keystone role that the FLC model has played in the successful efforts that a small state agency has made in establishing pedagogically robust and technologically enhanced programs, courses, modules, and learning objects across twenty-four institutions. This is a model that all state agencies should consider.

In a vibrant and successful FLC program, there may be more than ten FLCs running at the same time. Connecting these efforts to an institution's teaching and learning center can provide a holistic, consistent, and exciting approach to faculty development. As Barton and Richlin describe in Chapter Seven, managing multiple FLCs requires a blend of technical savvy for tracking budgets, Web sites, schedules, and audiovisual equipment and an optimist's cheerful and pampering spirit.

Assessment results provide the justification for investing time, effort, and funds in an FLC program. Faculty, administrators, facilitators, and students deserve to know the outcomes of FLC participation and its impact on growth, learning, and change. In Chapter Eight, Hubball, Clarke, and Beach bring Canadian and U.S. perspectives on the assessment of FLCs. In Chapter Nine, Vaughan looks at the role of technology in supporting inquiry cycles in an FLC and reports on a pilot test at his college using a community of inquiry model to facilitate reflection and critical discourse.

In Chapter Ten, Petrone draws on the reflective, double-loop nature of FLCs to show that they are an effective way to address institutional diversity issues and opportunities. She offers the lessons learned from facilitating a possibly risky and rewarding topic-based FLC over three years: the "dreaded diversity discussion" (Frederick, 1995) and explains ten factors that should be considered when including a diversity component in FLCs.

In order for the scholarship of teaching and learning to have a chance at acceptance, we knew that it had to approximate the rigors of disciplinary scholarship, including refereed presentations and publications (Richlin and Cox, 1991). We have carried that belief into the FLC approach. In Chapter Eleven, we describe how scholarly teaching and the scholarship of teaching can be developed in FLCs and are a key requirement for acceptance of FLCs in higher education.

In Chapter Twelve, Blaisdell and Cox discuss the yin and yang of working with midcareer and senior faculty in an FLC where teaching habits formed over years can be re-envisioned and the quest for learning taken up anew.

In Chapter Thirteen, Richlin and Essington report on adapting Preparing Future Faculty (PFF) programs to an FLC approach, and vice versa. Adding the community aspect to PFF programs provides a dimension that has been reported absent from graduate programs in recent studies. The authors also discuss the advantages of including graduate students in FLCs.

This volume brings a message of encouragement, wisdom, opportunity, and challenge to those contemplating, initiating, managing, or facilitating FLCs at their institution. Now we turn to the chapters written by our colleagues in celebration of faculty community. Read, reflect, and seek direction in your own communities. And if you do not have such communities in your college or university, then organize and build. We will assist you as you begin and as your FLCs evolve. Welcome to our community of those who build and lead faculty learning communities.

Milton D. Cox
Laurie Richlin
Editors

References

Angelo, T. A. "Transforming Departments into Productive Learning Communities." In A. F. Lucas and others (eds.), *Leading Academic Change: Essential Roles for Department Chairs.* San Francisco: Jossey-Bass, 2000.

Boyer, E. *Campus Life: In Search of Community.* San Francisco: Carnegie Foundation for the Advancement of Teaching, 1990.

Dewey, J. *How We Think.* Lexington, Mass.: Heath, 1933.

Frederick, P. "Walking on Eggs: Mastering the Dreaded Diversity Discussion." *College Teaching,* 1995, 43(3), 83–92.

Gabelnick, F., MacGregor, J., Matthews, R. S., and Smith, B. L. *Learning Communities: Creating Connections Among Students, Faculty, and Disciplines.* New Directions for Teaching and Learning, no. 41. San Francisco: Jossey-Bass, 1990.

McDonald, W. M., and others (eds.). *Creating Campus Community.* San Francisco: Jossey-Bass, 2002.

Meiklejohn, A. *The Experimental College.* New York: HarperCollins, 1932.

Palmer, P. J. "The Quest for Community in Higher Education." In W. M. McDonald and Associates (eds.), *Creating Campus Community.* San Francisco: Jossey-Bass, 2002.

Richlin, L., and Cox, M. D. "The Scholarship of Pedagogy: A Message from the Editors." *Journal on Excellence in College Teaching,* 1991, 2, 1–8.

Shulman, L. S. "Teaching as Community Property: Putting an End to Pedagogical Solitude." *Change,* Nov.–Dec. 1993, pp. 6–7.

Waller, W. *Sociology of Teaching.* New York: Wiley, 1932.

MILTON D. COX is director of the Center for the Enhancement of Learning and Teaching at Miami University, where he founded and directs the Lilly Conference on College Teaching, is editor-in-chief of the Journal on Excellence in College Teaching, *and facilitates the Hesburgh Award–winning Teaching Scholars Faculty Learning Community.*

LAURIE RICHLIN, director of the Claremont Graduate University Preparing Future Faculty and faculty learning communities programs, also is director of the Lilly Conference on College and University Teaching–West, executive editor of the Journal on Excellence in College Teaching, *and president of the International Alliance of Teacher Scholars.*

Faculty learning communities create connections for isolated teachers, establish networks for those pursuing pedagogical issues, meet early-career faculty expectations for community, foster multidisciplinary curricula, and begin to bring community to higher education.

Introduction to Faculty Learning Communities

Milton D. Cox

> The growth of any craft depends on shared practice and honest dialogue among the people who do it. We grow by trial and error, to be sure—but our willingness to try, and fail, as individuals is severely limited when we are not supported by a community that encourages such risks.
>
> —Palmer, 1998, p. 144

Community is playing an increasing and important role in our classrooms and institutions, connecting us with our students and colleagues (Cox, 2002). However, this growth has been slow, and there are many obstacles to implementation (Palmer, 2002). Creating a faculty learning community program is one approach that engages community in the cause of student and faculty learning and of transforming our institutions of higher education into learning organizations (Cox, 2001).

Community has played an important role in the development of the United States. Alexis de Tocqueville, visiting the new country in the 1830s to determine the reasons for the success of democracy, concluded that it was a result of the social capital—"the ways our lives are made more productive by social ties" (Putnam, 2000, p. 19)—generated by Americans of all dispositions who were very active in forming and participating in local associations. However, community has faced barriers, as noted by Putnam (2000) in his findings and concerns about the collapse of small, traditional communities during the last third of the twentieth century. With this all-too-brief comment about community in U.S. culture, we turn to needs for community in higher education.

NEW DIRECTIONS FOR TEACHING AND LEARNING, no. 97, Spring 2004 © Wiley Periodicals, Inc.

The isolation of college teachers in the 1920s was reported by Waller (1932). Even now, "The heart of the crisis in American education is the lonely work of teachers who often feel disconnected from administrators, colleagues, and many of their students" (Baker, 1999, p. 95). For example, in interviews with a random sample of 120 professors regarding their work as teachers and researchers, Baker and Zey-Ferrell (1984) noted distinct patterns: Research work involved elaborate and strong networks of support and collaboration, while teaching did not. There were two types of lonely teachers: the *splendid isolationists*—rugged individualists who were the best teachers in their department and expressed no need to consult about teaching—and *demoralized loners,* who consulted with no one because of bitter disappointments about students and colleagues.

Learning Communities

Boyer (1990) described colleges and universities as learning communities, which he characterized as purposeful, open, just, disciplined, caring, and celebrative. In higher education, the term *learning community* has many meanings. Baker (1999) uses the term to mean "a relatively small group that may include students, teachers, administrators, and others who have a clear sense of membership, common goals, and opportunity for extensive face-to-face interaction" (p. 99). He notes that classes, committees, advisory groups, interdisciplinary teaching teams, departments, and residential colleges have the potential to be—but may not be—learning communities. In some cases, the likelihood of having community is small. Duffy and Jones (1995) note that community in classrooms is a great opportunity that is often missed opportunity and that, if community is to be established, it needs to be done early in the term. Palmer (2002) comments: "Students are gathered in one place, called the classroom, not for the sake of community, but merely to make it unnecessary for the professor to deliver the information more than once" (p. 185). Palloff and Pratt (1999) describe requirements and methods for building virtual communities in cyberspace, noting that relationships established there can be stronger than those in face-to-face groups. A national study of departments found collegiality to be "hollowed" (Massy, Wilger, and Colbeck, 1994), with community usually absent from meetings, curricular planning, and pedagogical work. Angelo (2000) suggests ways to transform departments into learning communities, and Senge (2000) reports that department chairs, as local line leaders, must model the behavior necessary to build community. In learning communities, all members of the group are learners, and the group is organized to learn as a whole system (Baker, 1999).

Student Learning Communities

In order to understand faculty learning communities (FLCs), it is helpful to look at student learning communities (SLCs).

Background. The search for student community in higher education (Dewey, 1933; Meiklejohn, 1932) started long before Boyer's search for community in campus life (Boyer, 1990). In the 1920s and 1930s, Dewey and Meiklejohn became concerned about the specialization and isolation of faculty and curriculum in departments and disciplines. To address the absence of active and student-centered learning (Dewey, 1933) and a coherent curriculum connecting disciplines (Meiklejohn, 1932), they independently proposed the concept of cohorts of students taking courses in common across disciplines. This approach sputtered for fifty years, with flashes of success at a few institutions (Tussman, 1969) quickly followed by dissolution of programs unable to surmount various obstacles in academe. The student learning community movement finally was solidly established at Evergreen State University (Jones, 1981), then at other institutions in the state of Washington and across the United States.

Institutions have incorporated variations of five SLC models that differ in complexity, faculty involvement, and residential components. Gabelnick, MacGregor, Matthews, and Smith (1990) provide an excellent explanation of the five models, including the roles, challenges, and successes of faculty and students. The community formed by a student cohort plays a key role in achieving better student learning outcomes for students in SLCs compared with those who are not in SLCs.

Student Learning Community Outcomes. Tinto (1995) and MacGregor, Tinto, and Linbald (2000) review a compilation of assessment studies of SLCs and report promising results:

1. The support of a community aids retention. Students in SLCs, especially those at risk, underrepresented, and making C's and D's, fare better academically, socially, and personally.
2. Students' learning goes deeper, is more integrated, and is more complex. For example, student intellectual development (Belenky, Clinchy, Goldberger, and Tarule, 1986; Baxter Magolda, 1992; Perry, 1970) takes place at a faster rate, because students are exposed to ambiguity through opposite points of view in team-taught courses or a proseminar.
3. SLCs play an important role in faculty development. Faculty involved in SLCs achieve significant gains in personal, social, and professional development.
4. Sensitivity to and respect for other points of view, other cultures, and other people are enhanced for both students and faculty.
5. Civic contributions such as participation in student government and in service learning programs are higher.

In answer to the questions "Why learning communities? Why now?" Cross (1998) gives three reasons: "*philosophical* (because learning communities fit into a changing philosophy of knowledge), *research based* (because learning communities fit what research tells us about learning), and *pragmatic* (because learning communities work)" (p. 10).

But like general society (Putnam, 2000), higher education has barriers to community. As some faculty members attempt to move institutions from the instruction paradigm to the learning paradigm (Barr and Tagg, 1995), SLCs provide an example of just how difficult the learning paradigm is to implement (Barr, 1998). Registrars, department chairs, and faculty find it challenging to deal with tasks such as scheduling a cohort of students, rewarding team teaching, and teaching outside of one's department. Shapiro and Levine (1999, jacket) note: "When campuses begin to implement learning communities, whether they know it or not, they are embarking on a road that leads to a profound change in culture." Unfortunately, "learning communities always seem to push against an institutional glacier that grinds away at innovation, smoothing it out and trying to make it like everything else" (Gabelnick, MacGregor, Matthews, and Smith, 1990, p. 92).

Faculty Learning Communities

After the major research on learning outcomes in SLCs was published in the 1990s, we at Miami University noted similar outcomes in our faculty development program, in which groups of eight to twelve faculty members spent a year working on teaching and learning topics (Cox, 2000). As a result, we renamed these groups *faculty learning communities*. For a history of FLCs, see Cox (2002).

Definition of an FLC. At Miami University, we define an FLC as a cross-disciplinary faculty and staff group of six to fifteen members (eight to twelve members is the recommended size) who engage in an active, collaborative, yearlong program with a curriculum about enhancing teaching and learning and with frequent seminars and activities that provide learning, development, the scholarship of teaching, and community building. A participant in a Miami University FLC may select a focus course or project in which to try out innovations, assess student learning, and prepare a course or project mini-portfolio; engage in biweekly seminars and some retreats; work with student associates; and present project results to the campus and at national conferences.

There are two categories of FLCs: cohort-based and topic-based. Cohort-based FLCs address the teaching, learning, and developmental needs of an important group of faculty or staff that has been particularly affected by the isolation, fragmentation, stress, neglect, or chilly climate in the academy. The curriculum of a cohort FLC is shaped by the participants to include a broad range of teaching and learning areas and topics of interest to them. Five examples of cohorts with FLCs are junior faculty, midcareer and senior faculty, department chairs, deans, and graduate students preparing to be future faculty. More details about cohort FLCs are given in Chapter Two of this volume.

Each topic-based FLC has a curriculum designed to address a special campus teaching and learning need, issue, or opportunity. Faculty and professional staff members propose topics to the FLC program director, who then advertises a call for applications across the university. These FLCs offer membership and provide opportunities for learning across all faculty ranks and cohorts and make appropriate professional staff members available to focus on a specific theme. A particular topic may be new and involve an FLC for one or many years, ending when the teaching opportunity, interest, or issue of concern has been satisfactorily addressed. Topics addressed by these FLCs are listed in Chapter Two.

Our FLCs offer a more structured and intensive program than most groups of faculty that meet and work on teaching and learning issues, such as teaching circles (Quinlan, 1996), book clubs, seminars, or brown-bag luncheon discussion groups. Of course, if certain components, such as projects and community, are present, those types of groups may also be FLCs. Research teams long have been disciplinary groups that work together on discovery scholarship, but they may proceed without an emphasis on community. Multidisciplinarity and community are the elements that allow FLCs to excel in teaching and learning pursuits. An FLC is a particular kind of community of practice (Wenger, McDermott, and Snyder, 2002).

FLCs are different from, but in many ways like, most action learning sets (ALSs) in that they are "a continuous process of learning and reflection, supported by colleagues, with an intention of getting things done" (McGill and Beaty, 2001, p. 11). Both FLCs and ALSs are more than just a seminar series, committee, project team, or support, self-development, or counseling group. FLCs and ALSs have several aspects in common. Both meet for a period of at least six months; have voluntary membership; meet at a designated time and in an environment conducive to learning; treat individual projects in the same way with the group contributing suggestions and a timely schedule to completion; employ the Kolb (1984) experiential learning cycle; develop empathy among members; operate by consensus, not majority; develop their own culture, openness, and trust; engage complex problems; energize and empower participants; have the potential of transforming institutions into learning organizations; and are holistic in approach. FLCs differ from ALSs in that FLCs are less formal; for example, they do not focus extensively on negotiated timing of discussions or other formal structures at meetings. FLCs concentrate less on efficiency and more on the social aspects of building community; off-campus retreats and conferences include times for fun, and some gatherings during the year include family and guests. FLCs place more emphasis on the team aspect of support (while still consulting on each individual's project) and on the ultimate beneficiaries of the program: the students in the participants' courses and students participating as FLC associates (Cox and Sorenson, 1999).

Goals of FLCs. The long-term goals of an FLC program at most institutions are similar to those at Miami University:

- Build universitywide community through teaching and learning
- Increase faculty interest in undergraduate teaching and learning
- Investigate and incorporate ways that diversity can enhance teaching and learning
- Nourish the scholarship of teaching and its application to student learning
- Broaden the evaluation of teaching and the assessment of learning
- Increase faculty collaboration across disciplines
- Encourage reflection about general education and the coherence of learning across disciplines
- Increase the rewards for and prestige of excellent teaching
- Increase financial support for teaching and learning initiatives
- Create an awareness of the complexity of teaching and learning

FLC Outcomes. Paralleling the student learning community outcomes listed earlier in this chapter are the following results for Miami University (MU) faculty in FLCs:

1. Pretenure faculty are at risk for stress-related health problems and not acquiring tenure (Sorcinelli, 1992). As reasons, they cite a lack of community, the disconnect between their personal and academic lives, and incomprehensible tenure systems (Rice, Sorcinelli, and Austin, 2000). However, the pretenure faculty in MU's Teaching Scholars Faculty Learning Commmunity shared talk and advice about how to achieve tenure, reduce stress, and integrate family and academic worlds. Members of this FLC were tenured at a significantly higher rate than MU faculty who were not members (Cox, 1995). While one cannot claim that FLC participation was the reason for obtaining tenure, it is easy to see that a yearlong, intensive program on teaching, learning, and community did not harm their chances, a view that has been expressed by some department chairs in this research-intensive institution.

2. Faculty in MU's FLCs move quickly through stages of intellectual development in the area of teaching and learning (Cox, forthcoming). For example, many faculty members begin their academic careers as dualists (Perry, 1970) or in silence (Belenky, Clinchy, Goldberger, and Tarule, 1986), unaware of the scholarship of teaching and knowing only one way to teach. They see the authorities as experts who make the teaching evaluation instruments used in their department or division. FLC participants encounter and learn to embrace ambiguity through multidisciplinary perspectives and an increasing awareness of differing teaching and learning styles.

3. FLCs play an important role in faculty and student development. MU's FLC Program has twice (in 1994 and 2003) received Hesburgh Award recognition as an excellent faculty development program that

increases undergraduate learning. MU's FLC model has also been adapted by other institutions (see Chapters Two and Six).

4. In FLCs, sensitivity to and respect for other points of view, other cultures, and other people are enhanced for both faculty and students. In assessment of the impact of FLCs on the participants' faculty development outcomes, the reported rating across all FLCs with respect to "your awareness and understanding of how difference may influence and enhance teaching and learning" was 7.6 on a scale from 1 (very weak impact) to 10 (very strong impact) (Cox, 2002). The Faculty Learning Community on U.S. Cultures Course Development, involving ten participants designing seven courses, completed the task in 1.5 years, resulting in six courses approved for scheduling. The group collaborated on strategies for working with chairs and curriculum committees to get courses approved and offered (Heuberger and others, 2003).

5. FLC graduates make more civic contributions than those who have not been in FLCs. For example, a greater percentage serve as members of the University Senate, department chairs, and mentors for pretenure faculty (Cox, 2001).

Evidence That FLCs Work. At MU, evidence that student and faculty learning is improved through FLCs is found in the analysis of student learning that appears in the participants' course miniportfolios, in the results of teaching projects, and in final reports. Evidence documenting improvement in undergraduate learning outcomes is given in the results of surveys of fifty past FLC participants who reported (1) how and the degree to which student learning in their courses changed as a result of faculty learning community participation, (2) how they knew that it changed, (3) what processes or approaches resulted in increased learning, (4) the categories of their FLC teaching projects and the degree to which learning changed as a result of those projects, and (5) the degree of change in student learning due to a change in faculty attitude as a result of FLC participation. The learning objectives were categorized using the Angelo and Cross (1993) Teaching Goals Inventory. The degree to which student learning changed was rated as 0 (students learned less), 1 (no change), 2 (learned more to a small degree), 3 (learned more to a medium degree), or 4 (learned more to a great degree). Some highlights of the results follow, and more details are in Cox (2004):

1. An increase in students' "ability to apply principles and generalizations already learned to new problems and solutions" was reported by 94 percent of the respondents (average of the reported degrees of change is 3.0 on the 4-point Likert scale). The same results were reported for students' "ability to ask good questions" and their "ability to develop an openness to new ideas"; 96 percent reported an increase in students'

ability "to work productively with others" (3.2); 92 percent reported an increase in students' capacity to think for themselves (3.0); and 98 percent reported an increase in students' "ability to synthesize and integrate information and ideas" (3.1).

2. Respondents reported that they were aware that student learning had increased because of the successful achievement of existing (62 percent) or new or more (58 percent) learning objectives; better class discussion or engagement (84 percent); greater student interest (64 percent); better classroom atmosphere or engagement (68 percent); more positive student evaluation comments (54 percent); and better papers or other writing assignments (52 percent).

3. Reported approaches that resulted in increased learning (and their average degree of change) included cooperative or collaborative learning (92 percent; 3.0), active learning (92 percent; 3.1), discussion (88 percent; 3.1), student-centered learning (84 percent; 3.0), writing (82 percent; 2.7), and technology (74 percent; 2.6).

4. The average rating for the degree to which student learning increased as a result of participants' FLC teaching projects was 2.9 out of 4.

5. The percentage of faculty respondents indicating a change in student learning due to a change in the faculty member's attitude as a result of FLC participation (listed by type of faculty attitude, with the degree of change indicated after the percentage) was as follows: general enthusiasm about teaching and learning (98 percent; 3.3); scholarly teaching and the scholarship of teaching (92 percent; 3.2); being more reflective (94 percent; 3.2); being more comfortable (88 percent; 2.9); being more confident (90 percent; 2.8); being revitalized (90 percent; 2.7).

FLCs are also successful at changing or providing new curricula. At Miami University, the Faculty Learning Community Revising the American Studies Curriculum received a grant from the National Endowment for the Humanities and the next year received the Provost's Award for Best Program Review. Members of the Faculty Learning Community Integrating the Arts and the Curriculum have added various modules and perspectives to their courses (Reed and others, 2003), and participants in the Faculty Learning Community on Ethics Across the Honors Curriculum each developed a course in his or her discipline that contains a significant degree of ethical inquiry and that is offered for honors credit at least three times over a five-year period.

Over 10 percent of Miami University's faculty participate voluntarily in FLCs each year. There were eleven FLCs in 2002–03 and ten in 2003–04. A complete list of the eighty-one Miami University FLCs (twenty-three types) that have been implemented over the lifetime of the FLC Program (1979–80 through 2003–04) is available from Miami University (Cox, 2004, or http://www.units.muohio.edu/flc/flcdesc.shtml). One third of Miami University faculty have participated in FLCs, a percentage that remains constant as faculty come and go, a kind of institutional faculty community quotient. This implies that two thirds of Miami University faculty do not find the FLC approach attractive or feasible. This may be due to a lack of awareness, a greater commitment to individual disciplinary research and scholarship, a discomfort with or disinterest in working in a community, or lack of time to invest in the commitment. Even some of the faculty members who are working on individual projects join FLCs, because they find that results can be obtained faster, more efficiently, and with greater insights when shared with supportive and inventive colleagues in an FLC (see Chapters Eleven and Twelve).

State and National Dissemination of the FLC Model. In 1999, MU received a grant from the Ohio Board of Regents to encourage adaptation of MU's FLC for junior faculty by Ohio institutions. The Ohio Teaching Enhancement Program (OTEP) was initiated to accomplish this project (Cox and Jeep, 2000). By 2001, seven institutions had implemented successful variations of such FLCs, and more institutions have joined OTEP and created FLCs since.

In 2001, following its success in Ohio institutions, MU received a three-year grant from the Fund for the Improvement of Post-Secondary Education (FIPSE) to mentor the development of FLCs at five adapting institutions: Claremont Graduate University and Consortium, Kent State University, Indiana University–Purdue University Indianapolis, The Ohio State University, and the University of Notre Dame. In the third year of the grant, 2003–04, the five institutions have implemented sixty FLCs of thirty-one different types. Twelve of the FLCs are cohort-based, and forty-eight are topic-based. Each institution initiated two or three FLCs in its first year in the program, four to six in the second year, and four to seven in the third year. As a result of the OTEP and FIPSE project successes, in 2002–03 the Ohio Learning Network, a state agency, adapted the FLC model to develop thirty-one FLCs on technology-related topics at thirty-two institutions of higher education (see Chapter Six). The FIPSE FLC project has spawned a growing interest in FLCs, and by 2003–04, a wide range of institutions have established various versions of FLCs (see Table 1.1). These are discussed in Chapter Two.

Need for FLCs. Why has the FLC model attracted so much interest? In addition to the needs for community in higher education that were described earlier in the chapter, recent studies have reconfirmed evidence of the need for community for graduate students and early-career, midcareer, and senior faculty.

Lovitts (2001) argues that student persistence is connected to integration into the life of a department and gives four reasons that graduate students leave doctoral study: the absence of community, lack of information about doctoral study and inability to navigate the system, disappointment with the learning experience, and an unsatisfactory adviser relationship. Learning communities for preparing future faculty provide the community,

Table 1.1. Number and Type of Faculty Learning Communities Established at Five Institutions Through FIPSE Grant

Type of Faculty Learning Community	Claremont Graduate University & Consortium Institutions	Indiana University-Purdue University Indianapolis	Kent State University	The Ohio State University	University of Notre Dame	Total
Cohort-Based						
Junior or Early-Career Faculty			3	3	1	7
Midcareer and Senior Faculty				2		2
Preparing Future Faculty	3					3
Topic-Based						
Electronic Technology (General)	1			1	1	3
Collaborative Technology			3			3
Online Teaching and Learning			1			1
Electronic Technology in Society					1*	1
Navigating the Information World			1			1
Scholarship of Teaching and Learning on Instructional Technology Impact		1* 2				3
Scholarship of Teaching and Learning (General)	1			1		2
Multicultural Course Transformation		1*				1
Multicultural Course Transformation in First-Year Learning Block Courses		3				3

Table 1.1. (Continued) Number and Type of Faculty Learning Communities Established at Five Institutions Through FIPSE Grant

Type of Faculty Learning Community	Claremont Graduate University & Consortium Institutions	Indiana University-Purdue University Indianapolis	Kent State University	The Ohio State University	University of Notre Dame	Total
First-Year Student Experience Great Starts: Connecting the Mosaic			2	2		4
Problem-Based Learning		2			1	3
Psychology of Learning	1					1
Faculty Work		1				1
Capstone Experience		2				2
Teaching Statistics					1*	1
Teaching Writing-Enriched Courses	1					1
Graduate Teaching Fellows to Be Leaders in Their Home Departments				3		3
Faculty and Future Faculty (including graduate students)			2			2
Advisory Group for Preparing Future Faculty		1				1
Teaching and Learning of Ethics in a Laboratory Setting					1	1
Tablet PC Initiative					1	1

Table 1.1. (Continued) Number and Type of Faculty Learning Communities Established at Five Institutions Through FIPSE Grant

Type of Faculty Learning Community	Claremont Graduate University & Consortium Institutions	Indiana University-Purdue University Indianapolis	Kent State University	The Ohio State University	University of Notre Dame	Total
Teaching Foreign Language					1	1
Integration of Catholic Social Thought					1	1
Professional Teaching and Training	2					2
Teaching Research Methods Across the Curriculum	1					1
Teaching Women's Studies Courses	1					1
Scholarship of Teaching and Learning on Assessment in Gateway Courses		1				1
Teaching and Learning in Large Classes		1	1			2
Total: 31 FLC Types	11	15	13	12	9	60

* FLC continued into a second year with the same participants.

information, and support needed to address these issues (see Chapter Thirteen).

In higher education, early-career faculty are arguably our most important human investment. A working paper of the American Association for Higher Education (AAHE), *Heeding New Voices: Academic Careers for a New Generation* (Rice, Sorcinelli, and Austin, 2000), reported on results of structured interviews with new faculty and graduate students preparing for faculty work. They were asked about their hopes and experiences and what would make a faculty career more resilient and self-renewing. The findings echoed the results of research done a decade before (Boice, 1992; Sorcinelli, 1992). The situation has not changed much. The study identifies three core, consistent, and interwoven concerns of prospective and early-career faculty: lack of a comprehensible tenure system, lack of community, and lack of integration of their academic and personal lives. The researchers reported: "Interviewees told us they want to pursue their work in communities where collaboration is respected and encouraged, where friendships develop between colleagues within and across departments, and where there is time and opportunity for interaction and talk about ideas, one's work, and the institution" (Rice, Sorcinelli, and Austin, 2000, p. 13). FLCs provide early-career faculty with opportunities for discussion as well as a community in which participants can explore together their tenure systems and options for integrated lives (Cox, 1995).

The AAHE report concludes with ten recommendations for good practice. The first four deal with establishing a more comprehensible tenure system; the next three call for one-on-one mentoring of graduate students and new faculty by senior faculty and department chairs; and the final three advocate support for teaching (provide model syllabi, encourage visits to the teaching center), disciplinary scholarly development, and a balance between professional and personal life. Remarkably, none of the recommendations speaks directly to forming community, another indication that higher education is not interested in or equipped to deal with the yearning expressed so eloquently by our early-career colleagues. The report itself says, "It's not that we don't know what to do, it's that we don't do what we know" (Rice, Sorcinelli, and Austin, 2000, p. 22). While the recommendations of the report address some of the faculty concerns, the concept of faculty learning community is not mentioned, and again, the barriers to community in higher education are exposed.

Is there a need for community among senior and midcareer faculty? Reporting on her study of midcareer faculty in a Canadian university, Karpiak (1997) found that one cohort experienced a malaise that included burnout and a need for renewal and found teaching unrewarding. This group felt isolated and on the periphery. The ten recommendations in this report (Karpiak, 1997) included three that spoke directly to forming community: promote among faculty a sense that they are involved in a joint enterprise and that they are members of a team; foster an environment in which colleagues stimulate one another's intellectual interests and help each other develop and grow; and develop support networks so that faculty know they are not alone—sponsored networks, wherein colleagues can offer support to others. An FLC program that includes an FLC for midcareer and senior faculty can accomplish these recommendations (see Chapter Twelve).

Qualities Necessary for Community in FLCs. Community is a key part of an FLC (Cox, 2002). Across institutions, the FLC program directors have found that the following ten qualities need to be present in an FLC to foster community and thus the process of synergistic knowledge development (Mu and Gnyawali, 2003). These qualities are listed in Appendix A.

Components of an FLC. At this point in FLC program development, the developers have identified thirty components of an FLC (Cox, 2002). The degree of engagement in the components selected for an FLC may vary, depending on the type of FLC and institution. As an institution's experience with FLCs increases, the degree of engagement with each component and the number of components involved will usually increase. When appropriate, the components should be considered both globally with respect to the overall FLC program and locally for each particular FLC. Examples, memos, and more details are in Cox (2004). The components are in Appendix B.

Conclusion

Community has not been included in survey questions or responses to determine existing or effective faculty development practices (Centra, 1978; Erickson, 1986; Kurfiss and Boice, 1990; Wright and O'Neil, 1995). Workshops and consulting can provide only surface or single-loop learning (acting to achieve a result without much deep reflection on value or appropriateness) for the participants, but an FLC provides deep, double-loop learning (careful reflection on the appropriateness of actions with respect to outcomes and social structures) for the topics that the participants address (Argyris, 1993). Thus, a member of an FLC on any topic will not only learn about that, but over the course of the year will design and implement it in a focus course, with many opportunities to reflect with other FLC participants on its effectiveness and the assessment of resulting student learning and feedback. An FLC program can include many bridges linking faculty to deep learning, early-career faculty to experienced faculty, isolated teachers to new colleagues, departments to departments, disciplinary curricula to general education, and faculty to students and staff. Through FLC programs at some point we will have established sufficient connections in our institutions to support a learning organization and overcome the isolation in higher education.

Appendix A: Qualities Necessary for Community in FLCs

1. *Safety and trust.* In order for participants to connect with one another, they must have a sense of safety and trust. This is especially true when participants reveal weaknesses in their teaching or ignorance of teaching processes or literature.

2. *Openness.* In an atmosphere of openness, participants can feel free to share their thoughts and feelings without fear of retribution.

3. *Respect.* In order to coalesce as a learning community, members need to feel that they are valued and respected as people. It is important for the university to acknowledge their participation by financially supporting community projects and participation at FLC topic–related conferences.

4. *Responsiveness.* Members must respond respectfully to one another, and the facilitator(s) must respond quickly to the participants. The facilitator should welcome the expression of concerns and preferences and, when appropriate, share these with individuals and the entire FLC.

5. *Collaboration.* The importance of collaboration in consultation and group discussion on individual members' projects and on achieving community learning outcomes hinges on group members' ability to work with and respond to one another. In addition to individual projects, joint projects and presentations should be welcomed.

6. *Relevance.* Learning outcomes are enhanced by relating the subject matter of the FLC to the participants' teaching, courses, scholarship, professional interests, and life experiences. All participants should be encouraged to seek out and share teaching and other real-life examples to illustrate these outcomes.

7. *Challenge.* Expectations for the quality of FLC outcomes should be high, engendering a sense of progress, scholarship, value, and accomplishment. Sessions should include, for example, some in which individuals share syllabi and report on their individual projects.

8. *Enjoyment.* Activities must include social opportunities to lighten up and bond and should take place in invigorating environments. For example, a retreat can take place off-campus at a nearby country inn, state park, historic site, or the like.

9. *Esprit de corps.* Sharing individual and community outcomes with colleagues in the academy should generate pride and loyalty. For example, when the community makes a campus presentation, participants strive to provide an excellent session.

10. *Empowerment.* A sense of empowerment is both a crucial element and a desired outcome of participation in an FLC. In the construction of a transformative learning environment, the participants gain a new view of themselves and a new sense of confidence in their abilities. Faculty members leave their year of participation with better courses and a clearer understanding of themselves and their students. Key outcomes include scholarly teaching and contributions to the scholarship of teaching.

Appendix B: The Components of an FLC

In the list below, no asterisk denotes a component that is the primarily the responsibility of an FLC facilitator. One asterisk denotes a component that is the primary responsibility of the FLC program director, and two asterisks denote components that are the responsibility of both.

Mission and Purpose
1. * Goals for the institution (What do you want the FLC program to accomplish?)
2. ** Objectives for each FLC (How do you plan to bring about the above goals through specific objectives for each FLC?)

Curriculum
3. * What FLCs to offer (cohorts, topics)
4. ** What issues and topics to address within each FLC

Administration
5. ** Facilitator qualities and criteria for the FLC program and for each FLC
6. ** Selection procedures and criteria for membership in each FLC (striking a balance among disciplines, needs, gender, experience)

7. ** Public relations (advertising each FLC, recruiting applicants, and publicizing FLC activities and accomplishments)
8. ** Financial support and budgets

Connections
9. Community (bonding within; support; safety)
10. ** Partnerships (bridging to and cosponsoring with other programs and units inside and outside the institution)
11. ** Engagement (serving the broader community: student and faculty organizations, K–12, statewide, and so on)

Affiliated Participants
12. ** Faculty or administrative partners (for example, mentors, consultants)
13. Student associates (for example, undergraduate peer mentors, teaching assistants, consultants)

Meetings and Activities
14. Seminars (length, frequency, topics)
15. Retreats (getting away; working and learning together)
16. Conferences (getting away; learning from others)
17. Social amenities and gatherings

Scholarly Process
18. The literature (articles, focus book)
19. Focus courses or projects (syllabus; teaching goals inventory; classroom assessment techniques; small group instructional diagnosis; pilot; assessment)
20. Individual teaching projects or other projects
21. ** Presentations, both on campus and at conferences (by individual members of the FLC or the entire group)
22. Course or project miniportfolio (prepared by each FLC member for his or her focus course or project)
23. Publication (usually in a year after the FLC)
24. The scholarship of teaching and learning

Assessment
25. ** Of faculty or staff development
26. * Of FLC program components
27. ** Of student learning in the classes or projects of FLC participants

Enablers and Rewards
28. ** Reassigned (release) time for participants and the FLC facilitator
29. ** Professional expenses for participants and the FLC facilitator
30. ** Recognition by the provost, deans, department chairs, colleagues

References

Angelo, T. A. "Transforming Departments into Productive Learning Communities." In A. F. Lucas and Associates (eds.), *Leading Academic Change: Essential Roles for Department Chairs.* San Francisco: Jossey-Bass, 2000.

Angelo, T. A., and Cross, K. P. *Classroom Assessment Techniques: A Handbook for College Teachers.* (2nd ed.) San Francisco: Jossey-Bass, 1993.

Argyris, C. *Knowledge for Action: A Guide to Overcoming Barriers to Organizational Change.* San Francisco: Jossey-Bass, 1993.

Baker, P. "Creating Learning Communities: The Unfinished Agenda." In B. A. Pescosolido and R. Aminzade (eds.), *The Social Works of Higher Education.* Thousand Oaks, Calif.: Pine Forge Press, 1999.

Baker, P., and Zey-Ferrell, M. "Local and Cosmopolitan Orientations of Faculty: Implications for Teaching." *Teaching Sociology,* 1984, *12,* 82–106.

Barr, R. B. "Obstacles to Implementing the Learning Paradigm." *About Campus,* Sept.–Oct. 1998, *3*(4), 18–25.

Barr, R. B., and Tagg, J. "From Teaching to Learning: A New Paradigm for Undergraduate Education." *Change,* Nov.–Dec. 1995, *27*(6), 13–25.

Baxter Magolda, M. *Knowing and Reasoning in College: Gender-Related Patterns in Students' Intellectual Development.* San Francisco: Jossey-Bass, 1992.

Belenky, M. B., Clinchy, B. M., Goldberger, N. R., and Tarule, J. M. *Women's Ways of Knowing: The Development of Self, Voice, and Mind.* New York: Basic Books, 1986.

Boice, R. *The New Faculty Member: Supporting and Fostering Professional Development.* San Francisco: Jossey-Bass, 1992.

Boyer, E. *Campus Life: In Search of Community.* San Francisco: Carnegie Foundation for the Advancement of Teaching, 1990.

Centra, J. A. "Types of Faculty Development Programs." *Journal of Higher Education,* 1978, *49*(2), 150–161.

Cox, M. D. "The Development of New and Junior Faculty." In W. A. Wright and Associates (eds.), *Teaching Improvement Practices: Successful Strategies for Higher Education.* Bolton, Mass.: Anker, 1995.

Cox, M. D. "Comparing Student Learning Communities and Faculty Learning Communities: Similar Successes, Similar Obstacles." Paper presented at the 12th annual Lilly Conference on College Teaching–West, UCLA Conference Center, Lake Arrowhead, Calif., Mar. 2000.

Cox, M. D. "Faculty Learning Communities: Change Agents for Transforming Institutions into Learning Organizations." *To Improve the Academy,* 2001, *19,* 69–93.

Cox, M. D. "The Role of Community in Learning: Making Connections for Your Classroom and Campus, Your Students and Colleagues." In G. S. Wheeler (ed.), *Teaching and Learning in College: A Resource for Educators.* Elyria, Ohio: Info-Tec, 2002.

Cox, M. D. "Proven Faculty Development Tools That Foster the Scholarship of Teaching in Faculty Learning Communities." *To Improve the Academy,* 2003, *21,* 109–142.

Cox, M. D. *Faculty Learning Community Program Director's and Facilitator's Handbook.* Oxford, Ohio: Miami University, 2004.

Cox, M. D. "Fostering the Scholarship of Teaching and Learning Through Faculty Learning Communities." *Journal on Excellence in College Teaching,* forthcoming.

Cox, M D., and Jeep, J. M. "Taking Your Best Faculty Development Program Statewide in the 21st Century: Mentoring Other Campuses Regarding Junior Faculty." Paper presented at the 25th annual conference of the Professional and Organizational Development Network, Vancouver, Canada, Nov. 2000.

Cox, M. D., and Sorenson, D. L. "Student Collaboration in Faculty Development: Connecting Directly to the Learning Revolution." *To Improve the Academy,* 1999, *18,* 97–127.

Cross, K. P. "Why Learning Communities? Why Now?" *About Campus,* July–Aug. 1998, 4–11.

Dewey, J. *How We Think.* Lexington, Mass.: Heath, 1933.

Duffy, D. K., and Jones, J. W. *Teaching Within the Rhythms of the Semester.* San Francisco: Jossey-Bass, 1995.

Erickson, G. "A Survey of Faculty Development Practices." *To Improve the Academy,* 1986, *5,* 182–196.

Gabelnick, F., MacGregor, J., Matthews, R. S., and Smith, B. L. (eds.). *Learning Communities: Creating Connections Among Students, Faculty, and Disciplines.* New Directions for Teaching and Learning, no. 41. San Francisco: Jossey-Bass, 1990.

Heuberger, B., Briscoe, M., Fitch, F., Greeson, L., Hieber, M., Hulgin, K., and Paternite, C. "It Takes a Faculty Learning Community: Creating and Implementing Innovative

Diversity Courses Through Interdisciplinary Dialogue." Paper presented at the 23rd annual Lilly Conference on College Teaching, Oxford, Ohio, Nov. 2003.

Jones, R. *Experiment at Evergreen*. Cambridge, Mass.: Shenkman, 1981.

Karpiak, I. E. "University Professors at Mid-Life: Being a Part of. . . . but Feeling Apart." *To Improve the Academy*, 1997, *16*, 21–40.

Kolb, D. *Experiential Learning*. Englewood Cliffs, N.J.: Prentice Hall, 1984.

Kurfiss, J., and Boice, R. "Current and Desired Faculty Development Practices Among POD Members." *To Improve the Academy, 9*, 1990, 73–82.

Lovitts, B. E. *Leaving the Ivory Tower*. Lanham, Md.: Rowman & Littlefield, 2001.

MacGregor, J., Tinto, V., and Lindbald, J. H. "Assessment of Innovative Efforts: Lessons from the Learning Community Movement." In L. Suskie (ed.), *Assessment to Promote Deep Learning: Insight from AAHE's 2000 and 1999 Assessment Conferences*. Washington, D.C.: American Association for Higher Education, 2000.

Massy, W. F., Wilger, A. K., and Colbeck, C. "Overcoming 'Hollowed' Collegiality: Departmental Cultures and Teaching Quality." *Change*, July–Aug. 1994, *26*(4), 11–20.

McGill, I., and Beaty, L. *Action Learning*. (2nd rev. ed.) Sterling, Va.: Stylus, 2001.

Meiklejohn, A. *The Experimental College*. New York: HarperCollins, 1932.

Mu, S., and Gnyawali, D. R. "Developing Synergistic Knowledge in Student Groups." *Journal of Higher Education*, 2003, *74*(6), 689–711.

Palloff, R. M., and Pratt, K. *Building Learning Communities in Cyberspace*. San Francisco: Jossey-Bass, 1999.

Palmer, P. J. *The Courage to Teach: Exploring the Inner Landscape of a Teacher's Life*. San Francisco: Jossey-Bass, 1998.

Palmer, P. J. "The Quest for Community in Higher Education." In W. M. McDonald and Associates (eds.), *Creating Campus Community*. San Francisco: Jossey-Bass, 2002.

Perry, W. J. *Forms of Intellectual and Ethical Development in the College Years*. New York: Holt, Rinehart, and Winston, 1970.

Putnam, R. D. *Bowling Alone: The Collapse and Revival of American Community*. New York: Simon & Schuster, 2000.

Quinlan, K. M. "Involving Peers in the Evaluation and Improvement of Teaching: A Menu of Strategies." *Innovative Higher Education*, 1996, *20*(4), 299–307.

Reed, R. A., Armstrong, E., Biran, M., Cowan, D., Fellows, D., Hill, K., Miller, E., and Pan, Y. "Integrating the Arts into the Curriculum: The Approach of a Faculty Learning Community." Paper presented at the 23rd annual Lilly Conference on College Teaching, Oxford, Ohio, Nov. 2003.

Rice, R. E., Sorcinelli, M. D., and Austin, A. E. *Heeding New Voices: Academic Careers for a New Generation*. New Pathways: Faculty Careers and Employment for the 21st Century Series, Working Paper Inquiry no. 7. Washington, D.C.: American Association for Higher Education, 2000.

Senge, P. M. "The Academy as Learning Community: Contradiction in Terms or Realizable Future?" In A. F. Lucas and Associates (eds.), *Leading Academic Change: Essential Roles for Department Chairs*. San Francisco: Jossey-Bass, 2000.

Shapiro, N. S., and Levine, J. H. *Creating Learning Communities: A Practical Guide to Winning Support, Organizing for Change, and Implementing Programs*. San Francisco: Jossey-Bass, 1999.

Sorcinelli, M. D. "New and Junior Faculty Stress: Research and Responses." In M. D. Sorcinelli and A. E. Austin (eds.), *Developing New and Junior Faculty*. New Directions for Teaching and Learning, no. 50. San Francisco: Jossey-Bass, 1992.

Tinto, V. "Learning Communities, Collaborative Learning, and the Pedagogy of Educational Citizenship." *AAHE Bulletin*, Mar. 1995, *47*(7), 11–13.

Tussman, J. *Experiment at Berkeley*. London: Oxford University Press, 1969.

Waller, W. *Sociology of Teaching*. New York: Wiley, 1932.

Wenger, E., McDermott, R., and Snyder, W. M. *A Guide to Managing Knowledge: Cultivating Communities of Practice*. Boston: Harvard Business School Press, 2002.

Wright, W. A., and O'Neil, M. C. "Teaching Improvement Practices: International Perspectives." In W. A. Wright and Associates (eds.), *Teaching Improvement Practices: Successful Strategies for Higher Education.* Bolton, Mass.: Anker, 1995.

MILTON D. COX is director of the Center for the Enhancement of Learning and Teaching at Miami University, where he founded and directs the Lilly Conference on College Teaching, is editor-in-chief of the Journal on Excellence in College Teaching, *and facilitates the Hesburgh Award–winning Teaching Scholars Faculty Learning Community.*

*This chapter reports the results of a series of surveys that
investigated the locations and attributes of FLCs,
including type of institution and FLC sizes, budgets,
participants, and activities.*

Overview of Faculty Learning Communities

Laurie Richlin, Amy Essington

During the past five years, an increasing number of faculty learning communities (FLCs) have been developed to foster instructional development. Some FLCs are for cohort groups, such as new or junior faculty, and others are for mixed faculty groups addressing teaching and learning topics of interest. This growth in the number of FLCs has been due in large part to the efforts of Milton Cox, who began a cohort FLC for junior faculty members in 1979 as part of a Lilly Endowment program at Miami University (MU), expanded that program to include eighty FLCs at MU since that time, and applied for, received, and administered regional and national grants to help other institutions create FLCs. The International Alliance of Teacher Scholars and Miami University have cosponsored three summer institutes, conducted by Milt Cox and Marty Petrone, involving over ninety participants interested in beginning FLCs on their campuses. In addition, over the past five years, Milt Cox has done workshops on creating FLCs at twenty-four campuses and thirty-nine conferences.

There appeared to be a growing interest from colleges and universities in the FLC model, but there was no way to know whether they had been successful in implementing FLCs. In order to find out how and where FLCs have been created, who is in them, how they operate, and to obtain

The authors thank Nathan Garrett, master's student in the School of Information Science at Claremont Graduate University, who patiently and precisely contacted survey respondents to clarify their data and who turned the data collected into useful information.

recommendations and feedback from members and facilitators, it was necessary to track the rapid spread of FLCs. This chapter reports the methods and results of that quest.

Method

The search for FLCs was conducted during the late summer and fall of 2003. It involved an iterative process to be certain that the information collected described actual FLCs and not other types of programs.

Finding Institutions with FLCs. The first task was to identify academic institutions that have FLCs. From a database of over twenty thousand faculty and administrators interested in college and university teaching, the investigators created a list of people whose information had been updated within the past ten years and who had an e-mail address on record. An e-mail invitation to have their FLCs included in a listing for this volume was sent on August 7, 2003, to 9,302 people on that list, as well as to the 1,194 members of the listserv of the Professional and Organizational Development Network (United States) and over seven hundred members of the listserv of the Society for Teaching and Learning in Higher Education (Canada). In response to that e-mail message, 168 people from 165 institutions indicated that there were FLCs at their institution and that they were interested in having them listed. Using SurveyMonkey (http://www.surveymonkey.com), we created and sent an online survey to the 168 respondents on August 19, 2003, asking for the following information: types of cohort-based and topic-based FLCs that the institution had before 2000 and between 2000 and 2003, current (2003–04) FLCs, and future FLCs; details of current FLCs, including the type (cohort-based or topic-based), title, facilitator, number of participants, frequency of meetings, approximate budget, planned activities, and beginning and ending dates for each FLC; and demographic information on the respondent.

There are several difficulties in identifying institutions with FLCs and obtaining data. The first is that there is no single type of office on all campuses that could be contacted. Some institutions had FLCs created and supported in more than one place on campus, and some respondents were not aware that there were additional FLC programs at their institutions, so we had more than one respondent from an institution providing information to us. Undoubtedly, some recipients may not have realized that they did have FLCs on their campuses, and those campuses are not represented. Many recipients passed the survey on to others at their institution whom they identified as being more likely to have information.

The second challenge is in the definition of an FLC. In the original inquiry and in the survey itself, an FLC was defined as "a group of faculty and staff (usually between six and fifteen, eight to twelve recommended) who engage in a year-long program with a curriculum about enhancing teaching and learning and with frequent seminars and activities that provide learning, development, and community building" (Cox, 2001). In spite of this, information was returned about student learning communities, faculty workshops and seminars, teaching circles, mixed programs (for example, faculty meetings with programs about teaching), other informal faculty communities of sharing, and groups that did not include stable membership or that met for less than a year.

A third problem was in the timing of the survey; the initial e-mail message was sent in late summer, when some FLCs for the coming year were still being developed and details were not yet available.

All three of these challenges were mitigated by follow-up contact with the respondents, which is described in the following section.

Additional Surveys. Three follow-up surveys were sent to people who responded to the first survey. The first survey, on topics addressed by various chapters in this volume, was sent to the ninety-six people who had responded by August 28, 2003. The second survey, on the impact of FLC participation on incorporating diversity into teaching, and the third survey, on incorporating the scholarship of teaching and learning in FLCs, were sent to respondents at the 132 institutions that were eventually identified as having FLCs.

Additional Topics. The first follow-up survey asked questions pertinent to topics addressed in other chapters in this volume: use of technology (Chapter Nine), factors that facilitated and hindered creating FLCs (Chapter Three), and how FLC facilitators were selected, trained, and supported (Chapter Four). Full responses were received from seventy institutions; these results are summarized in the applicable chapters of this volume.

Diversity. The second follow-up survey asked questions about the impact of FLC participation on incorporating diversity into teaching; the respondents were asked to send the request for feedback to participants in FLCs in prior years who would have had the opportunity to modify their teaching. The questions asked were as follows:

1. In what ways has your participation in an FLC contributed to your understanding of diverse ways of knowing and learning?
2. As a result of participating in an FLC, to what extent is your teaching informed by the identity dimensions of age, race, ethnicity, gender, religion, ability, class, and sexuality?
3. What specific alterations to your course curriculum, syllabus, classroom interaction strategies, and/or pedagogy have you made?
3a. Why?
3b. With what effect?

The results of this survey are included in Chapter Ten.

Scholarship of Teaching and Learning. The third follow-up survey asked respondents whether their FLCs incorporate scholarship of teaching and learning (SoTL) activities and, if so, which aspects they include. The list that was provided in the survey included course development, course redesign, teaching projects, on-campus and off-campus presentations, on-campus and off-campus publications, and teaching portfolios or course portfolios. An open-ended "other" category was provided for additional activities. The results are presented in Chapter Eleven of this volume.

Follow-up of Original Survey. Early respondents encountered technical problems with the original survey. The investigators dealt with technical issues and provided clarification of questions and definitions through individual, direct contact with the respondents.

Technical Problems. Several technical problems were identified and corrected on the original survey. The first round of surveys included questions about details for up to ten FLCs, but the SurveyMonkey program kicked out respondents after they had entered information for only two FLCs. Later, the survey program was fixed, and additional respondents were able to enter information for up to ten FLCs. Respondents who entered two FLCs on the first round of surveys were contacted to find out whether they had additional FLCs; if they did, that information was collected.

Survey Clarification Problems. More complicated was verifying that the information on the surveys was correct. In the historical/summary part of the survey, respondents were asked to identify the cohorts and topics for their FLCs over the years. In many cases, more 2003–04 cohorts and topics were identified on the summary question than were detailed in subsequent questions. The research assistant e-mailed or called all institutions that had given such responses and found the following confusion: if an FLC included multiple groups (for example, new faculty and veteran faculty), respondents indicated each of them as a cohort; if a cohort dealt with multiple topics (for example, technology, writing), respondents indicated each of them as a topic. This was clarified so that FLCs were listed only once on the summary chart.

FLC Definition Problems. As noted above, we provided a definition of faculty learning communities as part of both the invitation to participate and the survey itself. Some respondents who had indicated interest in having their programs listed realized when they received the survey that they did not qualify. Several of those wrote that they would like more information on FLCs; one stated that he "started one a few years back, but it fizzled" and another that "I would like to start a faculty learning community, but it is a slow process." Many responses described FLCs that varied from the definition in that they did not include faculty, were not yearlong, did not have a curriculum, or did not include community-building activities. Most of those that did not fit could be called workshops or seminar series open to any faculty member who wanted to participate. These were not included on the listing.

Results

Respondents were from thirty-three states and four Canadian provinces. The highest numbers of current (2003–04) FLCs were reported in Ohio, which has sixty-five FLCs, including the thirty-one sponsored by the

Ohio Learning Network (see Chapter Six). Indiana, with thirty-one, and California, with twenty-eight, were the next highest. Five institutions in those three states are in the third year of the program sponsored by a Fund for the Improvement of Post-Secondary Education (FIPSE) Dissemination Grant to Miami University to "quick start" FLCs on other campuses.

The largest number of respondents (sixty-eight) were from a faculty development office or center, followed by thirty-six from individual departments, seven from provost offices, and three from student learning centers. Respondents identified their roles, with the highest percentage (68.4 percent) identifying themselves as an FLC program organizer, followed by 57.9 percent as an FLC facilitator, 50.9 percent as an FLC program director, 48.2 percent as a "proactive administrator," 33.3 percent as a "cheerleader," 28.1 percent as an FLC participant, 20.2 percent as a fundraiser, and 16.7 percent as an FLC advisory committee member.

Historical Summary. The first questions we had were about the numbers and types of FLCs that had begun before 2000, were in place each year since, and were planned for the 2003–2004 academic year.

Cohort-Based FLCs. The percentage of respondents reporting that their institution had no cohort-based FLCs declined from 32.7 percent before 2000 to 9.0 percent during the 2003–04 academic year. Most prevalent before 2000 were programs for new and junior faculty, followed by midcareer and senior faculty, and future faculty. Although the numbers have increased in each category every year, the relative percentage has remained the same.

Topic-Based FLCs. The largest percentage of topic-based FLCs have been on the scholarship of teaching topics and technology topics. Other frequently occurring topics have been the college experience of first-year students, assessment, and writing. In addition to the topics listed on the survey, over 40 percent of respondents reported that they had FLCs on other topics.

2003–04 Faculty Learning Communities. To obtain up-to-date descriptions of FLCs, our main focus was on those FLCs currently in operation. These we separated by their 2000 Carnegie classification.

Number of FLCs, by Carnegie Classification. After the results were clarified through e-mail and telephone interviews, 132 institutions were identified as having a total of 308 FLCs operating during the 2003–04 academic year. As can be seen in Table 2.1, there are 65 cohort-based and 243 topic-based FLCs. Cohort-based FLCs are found primarily at doctoral/research and master's universities, with smaller numbers at general baccalaureate colleges and associate's colleges.

FLC Budgets, by Carnegie Classification. Table 2.2 shows the annual budgets of the 2003–04 FLCs by the Carnegie classifications of the institutions. There are 99 FLCs with budgets under $2,000, 76 with budgets over $10,000, 57 with budgets of $2,000 to $4,999, and 46 with a budget of $5,000 to $9,999. FLCs at doctoral/research institutions and baccalaureate colleges are equally likely to have a budget under $2,000 or over $10,000. FLCs at master's institutions are almost three times as likely to have a budget under $10,000 as over that amount.

Table 2.1. Number of FLCs, by Carnegie Classification

Carnegie Classification of Institution	Number of Institutions/Total in Category (Percentage)	Number of Cohort-Based FLCs	Number of Topic-Based FLCs	Total Number of FLCs
Doctoral/Research University—Extensive	38/151 (25.2%)	33	71	104
Doctoral/Research University—Intensive	14/110 (12.7%)	6	34	40
Master's College/University I	34/496 (6.8%)	8	59	67
Master's College/University II	7/115 (6.1%)	4	15	19
Baccalaureate College—Liberal Arts	3/225 (1.3%)	0	5	5
Baccalaureate College—General	6/324 (1.9%)	4	9	13
Baccalaureate/Associate's College	1/57 (1.7%)	0	4	4
Associate's College	16/1668 (.96%)	6	27	33
Specialized—Theological and Faith-Based	1/766 (.13%)	0	1	1
Specialized—Non-Medical Health Profession	1/97 (1.0%)	0	1	1
Specialized—Engineering and Technology	2/66 (3.0%)	0	2	2
Specialized—Other	2/71 (2.8%)	0	2	2
Total—U.S. Academic Institutions	125/4146 (3.0%)	61	232	291
Canadian College/University	5/402 (1.2%)	4	9	13
Not Applicable (Consortiums)	2	0	4	4
Total—All Institutions	132	65	243	308

Table 2.2. FLC Budgets, by Carnegie Classification

Carnegie Classification	Under $2,000	$2,000 to $4,999	$5,000 to $9,999	$10,000 or More	Undetermined/ Unknown	Total
Doctoral/Research University—Extensive	22	26	24	28	4	104
Doctoral/Research University—Intensive	8	11	6	11	4	40
Master's College/University I	32	7	8	13	7	67
Master's College/University II	12	5	0	2	0	19
Baccalaureate College—Liberal Arts	4	0	0	1	0	5
Baccalaureate College—General	2	2	2	5	2	13
Baccalaureate/Associate's College	0	1	0	3	0	4
Associate's College	12	4	2	5	10	33
Specialized—Theological and Faith-Based	0	0	0	0	1	1
Specialized—Non-Medical Health Profession	1	0	0	0	0	1
Specialized—Engineering and Technology	1	0	0	0	1	2
Specialized—Other	2	0	0	0	0	2
Canadian College/University	2	1	3	6	1	13
Not Applicable (Consortiums)	1	0	1	2	0	4
Total	99	57	46	76	30	308

Type of FLC, by Budget. Table 2.3 compares the budgets of cohort-based and topic-based FLCs. Of respondents who provided budget information, the highest percentage (35 percent) have budgets over $10,000, followed by under $2,000 (30 percent), $2,000 to $4,999 (17.5 percent), and $5,000 to $9,999 (17.5 percent). For topic-based FLCs, 37 percent have budgets under $2,000, followed by 25 percent with budgets over $10,000, 21 percent between $2,000 and $4,999, and 16 percent between $5,000 and $9,999.

FLC Activities, by Budget. Interestingly, FLCs with budgets under $2,000 had more seminars, social gatherings, and activities overall than FLCs with budgets between $2,000 and $9,999. FLCs with budgets $10,000 or more had fewer seminars than the FLCs under $2,000 but attended considerably more conferences and retreats. Table 2.4 shows the distribution of 644 activities listed by survey respondents.

Cohort-Based FLCs, by Carnegie Classification. Of the cohort-based FLCs listed in Table 2.5, almost half are for new or junior faculty and two-thirds of those are in master's and doctoral universities. A quarter of cohort-based FLCs are for preparing future faculty; others are for midcareer or senior faculty and department chairs.

Cohort FLC Participants, by Budget. Table 2.6 shows that the largest number of cohort FLCs fall within the "7–10 Participants" category. Not surprisingly, FLCs with higher budgets support the largest number of FLCs with more than fifteen participants. The category with the fewest FLCs is

Table 2.3. Type of FLC, by Budget

Budget	Cohort-Based	Topic-Based	Total
Under $2,000	19	80	99
$2,000 to $4,999	11	46	57
$5,000 to $9,999	11	35	46
$10,000 or more	22	54	76
Undetermined	2	8	10
Unknown	0	20	20
Total	65	243	308

Table 2.4. FLC Activities, by Budget

Budget	Seminars	Social Gatherings	Retreats	Conferences	Other	Total
Under $2,000	82	41	9	13	25	170
$2,000 to $4,999	53	37	23	16	6	135
$5,000 to $9,999	42	28	20	18	19	127
$10,000 or more	72	45	29	32	23	201
Undetermined	5	3	1	0	1	10
Unknown	0	0	0	0	1	1
Total	254	154	82	79	75	644

Table 2.5. Cohort-Based FLCs, by Carnegie Classification

Carnegie Classification of Institution	Department Chairs	Midcareer/ Senior	New/ Junior	Future Faculty	Other Cohort	Total
Doctoral/Research University—Extensive	1	4	12	11	5	33
Doctoral/Research University—Intensive	1	1	2	2	0	6
Master's College/University I	0	3	5	0	0	8
Master's College/University II	0	1	2	0	1	4
Baccalaureate College—Liberal Arts	0	0	0	0	0	0
Baccalaureate College—General	1	0	3	0	0	4
Baccalaureate/Associate's College	0	0	0	0	0	0
Associate's College	0	0	4	0	2	6
Specialized—Theological and Faith-Based	0	0	0	0	0	0
Specialized—Non-Medical Health Profession	0	0	0	0	0	0
Specialized—Engineering and Technology	0	0	0	0	0	0
Specialized—Other	0	0	0	0	0	0
Canadian College/University	0	0	2	2	0	4
Not Applicable (Consortiums)	0	0	0	0	0	0
Total	3	9	30	15	8	65

"6 or Fewer Participants." Most FLCs with seven to ten participants report having a budget of either under $2,000 or $10,000 or more.

Cohort FLC Meeting Frequency, by Budget. As shown in Table 2.7, most (almost 75 percent) of the cohort groups meet either every two weeks or once a month. FLCs with lower budgets are likely to meet less frequently than those with higher budgets.

Cohort FLC Activities, by Budget. Although the definition of an FLC includes having frequent seminars, 10.8 percent of cohort FLCs were described as not having any seminars (which begs the question of whether they actually are FLCs). Table 2.8 show that FLCs with budgets of $10,000

Table 2.6. Cohort FLC Participants, by Budget

	Participants					
Budget	6 or Fewer	7–10	11–15	More Than 15	Unknown	Total
Under $2,000	2	10	5	2	0	19
$2,000 to $4,999	1	4	4	2	0	11
$5,000 to $9,999	1	4	1	5	0	11
$10,000 or more	2	9	4	7	0	22
Undetermined	0	0	0	0	2	2
Total	6	27	14	16	2	65

Table 2.7. Cohort FLC Meeting Frequency, by Budget

	Meeting Frequency						
Budget	Every Week	Every Two Weeks	Every Three Weeks	Monthly	Other	Undetermined/ Unknown	Total
Under $2,000	2	6	0	10	0	1	19
$2,000 to $4,999	2	4	0	4	1	0	11
$5,000 to $9,999	2	2	2	2	3	0	11
$10,000 or more	2	10	0	9	1	0	22
Undetermined	0	0	0	0	0	2	2
Total	8	22	2	25	5	3	65

Table 2.8. Cohort FLC Activities, by Budget

	Activities						
Budget	Seminars	Social Gatherings	Retreats	Conferences	Other	Unknown	Total
Under $2,000	15	11	2	3	6	1	38
$2,000 to $4,999	10	9	4	4	0	1	28
$5,000 to $9,999	10	8	5	3	3	0	29
$10,000 or more	22	17	15	10	6	0	70
Undetermined	0	0	0	0	0	2	2
Total	57	45	26	20	15	4	167

or more reported more seminars, social gatherings, retreats, and conferences than those with lower budgets.

Topic-Based FLCs, by Carnegie Classification. Table 2.9 shows the number of topics being addressed by FLCs during 2003–2004. FLCs that reported focusing on general or specific teaching topics account for 76 (31.3 percent) of the topic-based FLCs; the three technology topics account for 38 FLCs (15.6 percent), and the scholarship of teaching for 24 FLCs (9.9 percent). Most topic-based FLCs are in doctoral (43.6 percent) and master's universities (30.0 percent), with the next most significant number in associate's colleges (11.1 percent).

Topic-Based FLC Participants by Budget. The highest number of topic-based FLCs (87, or 35.8 percent) fall into the "7–10 Participants" category, followed by "More Than 15 Participants" (25.5 percent) and "11–15 Participants" (20.6 percent). Almost half of the topic-based FLCs with a budget of $10,000 or more have more than fifteen participants, while only 22.5 percent of those with a budget under $2,000 are that large. More than half of the topic-based FLCs with budgets between $2,000 and $9,999 have seven to ten participants (Table 2.10).

Topic-Based FLC Meeting Frequency by Budget. As shown in Table 2.11, topic-based FLCs are most likely to meet monthly, followed by every two weeks and "other" intervals. A much lower percentage of topic-based FLCs (19 percent) than cohort-based FLCs (34 percent) meets every two weeks. More than twice the percentage of topic-based FLCs (9.8 percent) as compared with cohort-based FLCs (4.0 percent) had not yet set their meeting schedule at the time of the survey. Topic-based FLCs are more likely than cohort-based FLCs to have monthly meetings in every budget category.

Topic-Based FLC Activities, by Budget. Seminars are the most frequent activities for topic-based FLCs, comprising almost 40 percent of reported activities (Table 2.12). The second most frequent activity is the social gathering. As in cohort-based FLCs, social gatherings play a central role in topic-based FLCs. Figures for participation by topic-based FLCs in conferences, retreats, unknown, and other activities are comparable to those in cohort-based FLCs. Topic-based FLCs with a budget of $10,000 or more participate in significantly more retreats and conferences.

Staying Current

Two Web sites (one in HTML and the other a downloadable Excel file) have been established to provide and maintain an up-to-date listing of faculty learning communities. Each site includes a full listing by institution, a listing of cohort-based FLCs by cohort group, and a listing of topic-based FLCs by topic category.

HTML: http://www.cgu.edu/pff/FLCResearch/Word_html/FLCList.htm
Excel: http://www.cgu.edu/pff/FLCResearch/Word_html/FLCList.xls

Table 2.9. Topic-Based FLCs, by Carnegie Classification

Carnegie Classification of Institution	A	B	C	D	E	F	G	H	I	J	K	L	M	N	O	P	Q	R	S	T	U	Total
Doctoral/Research University—Extensive	1	2		4	2	3	1	7	8		4	1	4	2	13	2	12	1	1	2	1	71
Doctoral/Research University—Intensive		2	1	2				1	3	1	1		6	1	5	1	3	1	3	4		35
Master's College/University I	4	1	2	3	2	3	2	2	13		1		6	1	5	3	4		2	4		58
Master's College/University II	1	1				1	1		4			1	1		3			1		2		15
Baccalaureate College—Liberal Arts								1	1						1	1				1		5
Baccalaureate College—General				1				1	3				1		1		1		1			9
Baccalaureate/Associate's College				2					1		1											4
Associate's College	2	1	3			1	1	1	6		1		4		2	1	3		1			27
Specialized—Theological and Faith-Based																1						1
Specialized—Non-Medical Health Profession									1													1

Table 2.9. (Continued) Topic-Based FLCs, by Carnegie Classification

Carnegie Classification of Institution	Topic																					Total
	A	B	C	D	E	F	G	H	I	J	K	L	M	N	O	P	Q	R	S	T	U	
Specialized—Engineering and Technology															1	1						2
Specialized—Other									2													2
Canadian College/University	1	1						1	2				1		1		2					9
Not Applicable (Consortiums)		1	2										1									4
Total	9	9	8	12	4	8	5	14	44	1	8	1	24	4	32	10	25	3	8	13	1	243

Topics:

A—About Student Behaviors
B—Administration
C—Assessment
D—Cooperative Learning
E—Critical Thinking
F—Developing or Revising a Curriculum
G—Ethics
H—First-Year Experience
I—General Teaching Topics
J—Initiating a PFF Program
K—Problem-Based Learning

l—Research Methods
M—Scholarship of Teaching
N—Service Learning
O—Specific Teaching Methods
P—Technology (Distance/Web)
Q—Technology (General)
F—Technology (Specific Focus)
S—Diversity/Difference
T—Writing
U—Other Topic

Table 2.10. Topic-Based FLC Participants, by Budget

	Participants					
Budget	6 or Fewer	7–10	11–15	More Than 15	Undetermined/ Unknown	Total
Under $2,000	14	27	21	18	0	80
$2,000 to $4,999	4	29	5	8	0	46
$5,000 to $9,999	5	13	10	7	0	35
$10,000 or more	1	16	12	25	0	54
Undetermined	0	1	2	4	1	8
Unknown	0	1	0	0	19	20
Total	24	87	50	62	20	243

Table 2.11. Topic-Based FLC Meeting Frequency, by Budget

	Meeting Frequency						
Budget	Every Week	Every Two Weeks	Every Three Weeks	Monthly	Other	Undetermined/ Unknown	Total
Under $2,000	15	14	2	29	19	1	80
$2,000 to $4,999	5	14	1	17	7	2	46
$5,000 to $9,999	0	7	7	12	9	0	35
$10,000 or more	7	12	7	17	11	0	54
Undetermined	3	0	1	2	1	1	8
Unknown	0	0	0	0	0	20	20
Total	30	47	18	77	47	24	243

Table 2.12. Topic-Based FLC Activities, by Budget

	Activities						
Budget	Seminars	Social Gatherings	Conferences	Retreats	Other	Unknown	Total
Under $2,000	67	30	10	7	19	7	140
$2,000 to $4,999	43	28	12	19	6	0	108
$5,000 to $9,999	32	20	15	15	16	0	98
$10,000 or more	50	28	22	14	17	1	132
Undetermined	5	3	0	1	1	3	13
Unknown	0	0	0	0	1	0	1
Total	197	109	59	56	60	11	492

The sites will include FLCs developed in future years, and readers are encouraged to submit their information to pff@cgu.edu.

Reference

Cox, M. D. "Faculty Learning Communities: Change Agents for Transforming Institutions into Learning Organizations." *To Improve the Academy,* 2001, *19,* 69–93.

LAURIE RICHLIN is director of the Claremont Graduate University Preparing Future Faculty and faculty learning communities programs, director of the Lilly Conference on College and University Teaching–West, executive editor of the Journal on Excellence in College Teaching, *and president of the International Alliance of Teacher Scholars.*

AMY ESSINGTON is a doctoral candidate in American History at Claremont Graduate University and teaches history at California State University, Long Beach. She has been in three faculty learning communities and is cofacilitator of the 2003–04 FLC on Teaching Women's Studies Courses Across the Curriculum.

*For successful implementation of FLCs, consider
leadership recommendations for institutional change,
reasons for choosing the FLC model, and institutional
conditions that may facilitate or hinder FLC development.*

Institutional Considerations in Developing a Faculty Learning Community Program

Gary M. Shulman, Milton D. Cox, Laurie Richlin

Dear Faculty:

In recent years, we have been trying to change our institution. We did this because we were concerned about our future, so we kept searching for and finding one panacea after another. We have mandated many new programs related to issues of assessment, faculty roles and rewards, diversity, continuous quality improvement, posttenure review, student learning, and heaven knows what else. Anxious to find some way to improve our fiscal condition and institutional ranking, we imposed one program after another. We kept on changing while you went from neutral to skeptical to cynical to resistant because you perceived that all of these changes were just creating the illusion of progress toward some unclear or idiosyncratic goal. Now we have a significant number of the faculty unlikely to listen to our next idea, no matter how good it might be. For our contributions to this bleak state of affairs, we apologize.

—The Administration

Implementing Institutional Change

This satirical memo, inspired by Filipczak (1994), highlights the fact that educational institutions have experienced a dizzying number of new program initiatives in the last decade. Few of these changes last very long or deliver the hoped-for benefits, because they are met with half-hearted compliance, if not outright resistance, on the part of faculty members. High administrative turnover breeds a plethora of new initiatives as administrators seek to make their mark and climb to their next position by championing their current favorite program. The introduction of too many changes too quickly may lead to a coping strategy of hunkering down and waiting until a new administrator abandons a predecessor's favored program. If this cycle continues for an extended period, people may come to resist even programs that are clearly in their own best interest (O'Toole, 1996).

If this situation is present to even a modest degree, campus leaders must pause to consider whether it will be feasible to successfully establish a faculty learning community (FLC) program. Introducing FLCs represents a change from the status quo and may frustrate institutional members if it does not first address the reasons that people resist change. For example, an FLC will have a better chance of being accepted if other new programs on campus have been successful and the proponents are perceived as credible. If these two conditions are absent and are not addressed before launching an FLC, the probability for success will be lower.

Paralleling what Shapiro and Levine (1999) said about student learning communities, FLCs can profoundly affect campus culture and may represent a major institutional change. Thus, the institution's approach to managing change in general must be taken into account when considering whether and how to establish an FLC on campus. By addressing five key questions, an institution can gauge its commitment and capability to launch a new FLC program. The questions emerge from organizational change research (Kotter, 1996; O'Toole, 1996) and emphasize factors that will facilitate or hinder campus acceptance of FLCs.

Can the need for an FLC be established? Before formally implementing a new FLC program, key campus stakeholders must perceive a need to do so. The need can be established through conversations about opportunities to improve the teaching and learning process along with concrete benefits for doing so. It is more likely that a major new program will take root when the institution can create a sense of urgency to excel or identify a problem that can best be addressed using an FLC format. The program should not be framed as remedial or for faculty members who need fixing; participants should not be stigmatized. In essence, what needs to be said is "We can be even better in teaching and learning than we are now" or "We have to reach our full potential as soon as possible."

Leaders must determine whether there is sufficient evidence available to convince the campus community to consider committing to a new FLC program. Data that might suggest the need for FLCs include overall (not individual) teaching and learning assessment results, student satisfaction information, the desire for faculty to grow beyond their departments, and benchmark data from peer or aspiration institutions. The urgency of the need can be related to dates associated with upcoming accreditation review, the reporting of data for published institution rankings, campus satisfaction surveys, or other events. Accreditation agencies are now looking at faculty development programs and outcomes. Convincing evidence that the new FLC program addresses local needs will facilitate successful implementation. Evidence about the effects of FLCs on a variety of campuses appears in other chapters of this volume.

Can an FLC implementation team be sponsored? As Sandell, Wigley, and Kovalchick discuss in Chapter Four, a strategically appointed FLC implementation team has significant advantages over an individual or a weak committee that lacks the time or credibility to convince others. Mutual trust among members and a common purpose distinguish teams from weak committees and can be facilitated through carefully planned events characterized by candid conversation and through joint activities (for example, retreats, seminars, conference attendance). In effect, the team will be experiencing and then modeling the collaborative and supportive qualities associated with an FLC.

The institution must determine whether a team with the following four member characteristics can be constituted to facilitate making the FLC idea a reality. First, members should have sufficiently high position power so that those left off the team cannot easily block progress. Second, to ensure sufficient expertise, varied points of view should be represented (different disciplines, ranks, races, genders) so that informed, intelligent decisions will be made. Third, the team's credibility can be ensured by having enough people with a good reputation (informal influence and power) so that others will take its recommendations seriously. Finally, the team should have a sufficient number of experienced leaders who can attend to and balance the team's task and interpersonal needs. Leaders can be those with proven skills in either informal or formal roles.

Can a compelling FLC vision be drafted? Vision refers to an imagined picture of a desirable and feasible future that includes a rationale for why people should strive to create an institution where effective teaching and learning take place routinely. Other chapters in this volume provide information on specific FLC outcomes, processes, and strategies that can be adapted for a vision statement. An effective vision will make it abundantly clear what the purpose of the FLC is and provide guidance for making it part of the campus culture.

The vision creation process typically begins with an initial draft from an individual. The FLC implementation team then refines and models the vision over time. Other stakeholders may be included in the visioning process, which results in a statement that is desirable, feasible, flexible, and easily communicable.

Can the FLC vision be communicated? Ineffective or insufficient communication is one of the major reasons that organizational experts cite for failed change efforts (Boyett and Boyett, 1998; Kotter, 1996). The FLC vision and strategy should be repeated constantly through words and actions, in different campus settings, and in multiple media. Dialogue about the FLC is more persuasive than a monologue, so it is important to engage the key stakeholders in two-way conversation in order to build widespread commitment to the program.

Using the all-some-all technique incorporates this principle. All means giving everyone in the institution the opportunity to provide input. Some represents the FLC project team, which processes the input. All also represents informing everyone of the opportunities discovered by the input and the changes deemed necessary. This cycle needs to be repeated throughout the FLC creation and implementation process. Thus, the campus community is given the opportunity to influence program features and comment on the recommendations before they become final decisions. Of course, it is naïve to expect universal agreement on every detail. Having a voice in influencing outcomes, however, increases commitment to the overall program and ensures that it is customized to that particular campus's needs. The institution must determine whether it has the will and the resources to devote to this communication effort.

Can tangible progress be demonstrated quickly? Short-term tangible outcomes encourage continuation of the effort by providing evidence that the institution is on the right track. The FLC implementation team benefits from gathering data on the quality of their ideas. Openly rewarding and recognizing the people who contribute to making the change possible helps build support for the FLC program by turning ambivalents into supporters and resisters into ambivalents.

Acknowledging positive progress quickly makes it difficult for resisters to derail momentum or thwart supporters of the program. Thus, introducing FLCs on a limited basis by restricting the focus to a key issue or cohort will increase the probability that something positive will happen soon. Positive results will facilitate expansion of the foci and membership in FLCs later on.

Recommendations

If the answers to the five questions for determining institutional readiness for establishing the FLC program are not unambiguously positive, it is recommended that the initiative not be introduced until circumstances become more favorable.

Effective institutional change is based on "pull through," not "push through" thinking and design. Establishing an FLC program is like moving a string. If you push the string it may move but will likely bunch up. The direction of the movement is difficult to predict, and it will take time for the end of the string to feel any force at all. The "pull through" process involves leading people by permitting them to have influence from the beginning. Visualize how easy it is to move the string by using one finger to pull it along. The end of the string follows in the same direction as the beginning. Thus, the challenge for campus leaders is to devise an implementation strategy that pulls people toward voluntary FLC acceptance. It is easier to implement a change with people than a change to people.

In confronting the challenges of constant change and the need for enhanced teaching and learning, there is no substitute for FLC collaboration—people choosing to come together for a common purpose and willing to support one another so that all can progress. These values underlie both the desired end and the desired means for establishing a faculty learning community on campus.

Reasons to Choose an FLC Model: Becoming a Learning Organization

Senge (1990) describes a learning organization as one that connects its members closely to the mission, goals, and challenges of the organization. These close connections are necessary for the organization to meet the demands of rapid change. While faculty members often have such connections within their departments and disciplinary organizations, they usually do not make the broad interests of their institution a priority, partly because there are few institutional rewards for doing so; most rewards are department- and discipline-based. Rarely has a turf battle in a university senate meeting (when a quorum could be mustered) been resolved by the opponents offering to pause and consider the university's and students' best interests. As a result, faculty remain isolated from colleagues in other disciplines, and the curriculum remains fragmented. Thus, faculty members and students miss out on connections across disciplines. Campuswide action on many issues (except, perhaps, parking and salaries) flounders from lack of interest, involvement, and support.

Senge (1990) describes the five components of a learning organization as those that foster close connections among people within an institution. Patrick and Fletcher (1998) translate those components into behavior for the academy. Faculty learning communities produce team learning and community for their members (Table 3.1). FLC participants at Miami University rank "colleagueship and learning from other participants" as having the highest impact of all program aspects (Cox, 2002). Evidence that FLCs foster civic pride is found in participants' contributions in university leadership (Cox, 2001). Midcareer faculty malaise and marginalization are well addressed by FLCs (Cox and Blaisdell, 1995; Chapter Twelve of this volume). Revision of interdisciplinary curricula (for example, American studies) or integrating elements (such as the arts) into curricula (Reed and others, 2003) can be effectively accomplished by initiating such efforts using FLCs.

Table 3.1. Senge's Five Components of a Learning Organization and Ways That Faculty Learning Communities Develop Them

General Description (Senge, 1990)	*Transforming Colleges and Universities into Learning Organizations (Patrick and Fletcher, 1998)*	*Ways That Faculty Learning Communities Enable Senge's Five Components of a Learning Organization*
Systems Thinking View of the system as a whole, a conceptual framework providing connections between units and members; the shared process of reflection, reevaluation, action, and reward	Creation and recovery of a common language and processes across departments and divisions; setting and honoring institutional missions, goals, actions, and rewards	FLCs provide time, funding, safety, teams, and rewards to enable multidisciplinary participants to discover, reflect on, and assess pedagogical and institutional systems. Members discover and come to appreciate the synergy of connected campus units
Personal Mastery Support for individuals in achieving their maximum potential as experts in their field and addressing opportunities and problems in new and creative ways	Support for faculty to continue as experts in their discipline yet broaden their scholarship beyond discovery to include integration, application, and teaching, particularly multidisciplinary perspectives	Individuals develop teaching projects to address opportunities or shortcomings in their teaching and learning practice; receive a developmental introduction to the scholarship of teaching, with multidisciplinary perspectives; become expert teachers inside and outside their discipline
Mental Models Culture and assumptions that shape how an organization's members approach their work and its relationship to society; relationship of employees to the organization, peers, and clients	Change from a culture of autonomy and rewards for individual work to one of community building; rewards for faculty contributions to institutional goals and solutions of problems	Membership counters isolation and fragmentation in the academy. Members discover the high value of colleagueship across disciplines, develop appreciation of differences among students and their development; and begin to value students as associates and sojourners. Participation becomes an honor with financial rewards.

Table 3.1. (Continued) Senge's Five Components of a Learning Organization and Ways That Faculty Learning Communities Develop Them

General Description (Senge, 1990)	Transforming Colleges and Universities into Learning Organizations (Patrick and Fletcher, 1998)	Ways That Faculty Learning Communities Enable Senge's Five Components of a Learning Organization
Building a Shared Vision Collaborative creation of organizational goals, identity, visions, and actions shared by members; outcomes a result of teamwork, with each individual's contribution an integral part	Sharing of departmental and disciplinary visions across disciplines; identifying joint approaches to challenges such as implementing student learning communities, improving student learning, integration of technology, creation of an intellectual community	Members develop pedagogical goals and joint approaches in each community and share these with the campus to address challenges such as using technology in teaching, inclusiveness of classroom and curriculum, active learning, assessment of learning, discussion of campuswide issues, and taking positions and action
Team Learning Creation of opportunities for individuals to work and learn together in a community where it is safe to innovate, learn, and try anew	Colleges and universities with "learning communities for teaching and research with colleagues and students" (p. 162)	Team learning is the heart and purpose of a faculty learning community.

Forces, People, and Structures on Campus That Facilitate and Hinder the Creation of FLCs

As described in Chapter Two of this volume, a follow-up survey was sent on August 28, 2003, to the ninety-six respondents who had responded to the original survey on FLCs by that date. Seventy respondents (72.9 percent) provided feedback about their experiences in developing FLCs on their campuses.

Factors That Facilitate FLC Development. Interested faculty members and supportive administrators were mentioned as an important factor in successful FLC development by 84.2 percent of respondents. Following are some typical comments:

"A senior faculty member undergoing career transition from research to teaching and administration provided the critical organizational energy to get it going."

"Faculty teaching a course outside their area of expertise. We needed the community to offer support for the high degree of risk we were taking. "

"Faculty members who implemented learning teams following a workshop conducted on our campus."

"Department chairs across disciplines adjusted faculty loads to allow their faculty to participate as fellows."

"The chancellor's office, who encouraged us to engage a new group of faculty in residence in an FLC. "

Another important factor mentioned was the availability of funding, mentioned by 24.3 percent of respondents. Grants were received from institutions' states, the National Science Foundation, the Fund for the Improvement of Post-Secondary Education, the James Irvine Foundation, the Lilly Endowment, the Teagle Foundation, alumni, and various on-campus groups such as the honors programs and the diversity committees.

Faculty development professionals and centers were mentioned most often (57.7 percent) as leading players in FLC development. FLCs were recognized by several institutions as fitting into the overall development program outlined in their collegewide strategic plan.

Factors That Hinder FLC Development. Thirty-seven (52.9 percent) of the seventy institutions reported no "key forces, people, or structures on campus that most hindered the creation of an FLC" on their campus. Factors mentioned as hindrances were time, funding, inertia, promotion and tenure (and other) policies, "countervailing forces of a large, decentralized research university under financial stress," and "culture that undervalues time spent on teaching and learning improvement." Several also mentioned staff people and high administrators who, happily, have since been replaced.

References

Boyett, J., and Boyett, J. *The Guru Guide: The Best Ideas of the Top Management Thinkers.* New York: Wiley, 1998.

Cox, M. D. "Faculty Learning Communities: Change Agents for Transforming Institutions into Learning Organizations." *To Improve the Academy,* 2001, *19,* 69–93.

Cox, M. D. "The Role of Community in Learning: Making Connections for Your Classroom and Campus, Your Students and Colleagues." In G. S. Wheeler (ed.), *Teaching and Learning in College: A Resource for Educators.* Elyria, Ohio: Info-Tec, 2002.

Cox, M. D., and Blaisdell, M. "Teaching Development for Senior Faculty: Searching for Fresh Solutions in a Salty Sea." Paper presented at the 20th annual conference of the Professional and Organizational Development Network in Higher Education. North Falmouth, Mass., Oct. 1995.

Filipczak, B. "Weathering Change: Enough Already." *Training,* Sept. 1994, p. 23.

Kotter, J. *Leading Change.* Boston: Harvard Business School Press, 1996.

O'Toole, J. *Leading Change: The Argument for Values-Based Leadership.* New York: Ballantine Books, 1996.

Patrick, S. K., and Fletcher, J. J. "Faculty Developers as Change Agents: Transforming Colleges and Universities into Learning Organizations." *To Improve the Academy,* 1998, *17,* 155–170.

Reed, R. A., Armstrong, E., Biran, M., Cowan, D., Fellows, D., Hill, K., Miller, E., and Pan, Y. "Integrating the Arts into the Curriculum: The Approach of a Faculty Learning Community." Paper presented at the 23rd annual Lilly Conference on College Teaching, Oxford, Ohio, Nov. 2003.

Senge, P. M. *The Fifth Discipline.* New York: Doubleday, 1990.

Shapiro, N., and Levine, J. "Introducing Learning Communities to Your Campus." *About Campus,* 1999, *4*(5), 2–10.

GARY M. SHULMAN is a professor and interim chair of the Department of Communication at Miami University.

MILTON D. COX is director of the Center for Enhancement in Learning and Teaching at Miami University, where he has taught mathematics for over thirty years and where he directs the Lilly Conference on College Teaching.

LAURIE RICHLIN is director of the Claremont Graduate University Preparing Future Faculty and faculty learning communities programs and director of the Lilly Conference on College and University Teaching–West.

The processes for choosing, preparing, and supporting
facilitators for faculty learning communities are as
unique as the campuses housing them. This chapter
reports on a range of activities and highlights three
preparation programs.

Developing Facilitators for Faculty Learning Communities

Karin L. Sandell, Katy Wigley, Ann Kovalchick

Concerns about the successful integration of faculty within the university community prompt exploration of ways of establishing and building strong academic cultures. For many reasons, life in separate academic unit "silos" remains the norm for faculty and the academy. Emerging from the silos and building a new structure that nurtures the growth of an interdependent faculty culture remains a formidable task. One solution proposed by some institutions and individuals is the formation of faculty learning communities (FLCs), a strategy that parallels student learning communities (SLCs) in operation and purpose. Like SLCs, FLCs bring together diverse groups of individuals who share their experiences as they undertake common learning activities. In their development of community, their mutual perspectives and talents merge and become transformative, both for themselves and for the learning that takes place, as well as for the institution of which they are a part (Cox, 2001).

Most faculty members have had some chance to work with others in their institution through membership on a working committee. Distinctions between committees and FLCs remain critical to understanding why cultural change is a function of the latter. Both committees and FLCs may involve learning and community. For example, a recent presentation (Kalish, Harper, and Woodard, 2003) described an "accidental" learning community that occurred when a committee morphed into a community. But for an FLC, the attainment of both learning and community is the goal rather than a happy accident. Achieving that goal depends on a number of FLC components. One key to the process is the facilitator of the FLC.

There are further distinctions between committees and FLCs. A committee chair organizes meetings, creates an agenda, assigns tasks, monitors tasks, and connects with other individuals and groups in regard to the committee's charge. An FLC facilitator also may organize meetings and bring colleagues together, but the outcomes associated with FLC members' work are shaped through the interactions of their individual interests and abilities. The contrast in the titles of committee chair and FLC facilitator highlights the differences between the two. Chairs bring about order and direct outcomes, while facilitators help seed the conditions that allow for the growth of mutuality. While both chairs and facilitators probably can benefit from systematic study and preparation for their individual roles, developing good facilitation skills for an FLC remains particularly challenging (see Chapter Five).

Facilitator Selection, Preparation, and Support

Developing successful facilitators is approached in different ways by institutions supporting various types of FLCs on their campuses. As described in Chapter Two, questions on selection, training, and support of FLC facilitators were included in the follow-up survey sent on August 28, 2003, to institutions that had responded to the initial survey by that time.

Facilitator Selection. Survey respondents indicate that the largest number of FLC facilitators are faculty development professionals who have organized the FLCs themselves. Next are faculty members or professional staff members who have been recruited and appointed (often by the faculty development office) based on interest in the topic, followed by faculty volunteers who respond to notices about an FLC being developed. Many fewer facilitators are selected because they were prior members of an FLC (although this may increase as more FLCs are implemented), and the fewest go through an application and selection process (once again, through a faculty development office).

Facilitator Preparation. Almost 40 percent of responses indicate either that their institution does not prepare their facilitators or that the facilitators are in positions that already involve facilitation skills, such as faculty development professionals. For those that do provide training, the largest number provide their facilitators with documents and readings, followed by attendance at meetings, seminars, and conferences (both on and off campus). A few indicate that they have their facilitators visit campuses that already have FLCs.

Facilitator Support. Funding is the most frequent support given to FLC facilitators. The majority of funding is for materials and resources, with a small number of respondents indicating that they provide course release time to FLC facilitators. Other support includes project administration, such as assistance in scheduling meetings, symposia, and workshops; access to technology, such as listservs, WebCT, and computer labs; publicity and recognition (including counting FLC facilitation as "credit" for institutional service); attendance at off-campus conferences; and additional staff, often in the form of student support. Several respondents indicated that the facilitation was considered part of their normal course load or part of their job.

Purposeful FLC Facilitator Preparation Programs

We describe here three programs—one national and two campus-based—that have been specifically developed to prepare facilitators for their roles in leading FLCs.

National FLC Summer Institute. For the past four years (2000–2003), Milton D. Cox and Martha (Marty) Petrone have conducted a two-and-a-half day summer institute called "Designing, Implementing, and Leading Faculty Learning Communities: Enhancing the Teaching-Learning Culture on Your Campus." The ninety participants to date (twenty to thirty each year) came from fifty-three institutions in twenty-four states and one Canadian province. Teams of two to six people were sent by eighteen institutions. The institute process included the development of five-to-six-person communities with assignments and jigsaw groups, a cooperative learning structure in which members go to specialized small groups designed to explore FLC models, goals, objectives, activities, components, and types to develop skills they bring back to their home community. The communities began the process of initiating their own FLC programs by engaging in FLC activities such as focus-course syllabus development, teaching projects, exploration of new classroom assessment techniques, and assembling course miniportfolios.

One of the thirty-two learning objectives for the institute was the identification and selection of facilitators. Most of the participants who established FLCs on their campuses after an institute became a facilitator of at least one FLC. Those who have been unable to establish FLCs blame lack of funding. One person stated, "Unfortunately, I have not established an FLC. It was primarily due to severe budget cuts. . . . The administration decided to simply go the route of half-day meetings." Another reported, "I made an unsuccessful pitch to procure funding for an FLC for a junior faculty cohort during 2003–04. I'm currently making a pitch for the same thing for 2004–05. I'm not willing to run an FLC without the financial commitment to a course release for each member of the FLC, and that financial commitment has to come from higher up than me."

Participants whose campuses implemented FLCs report a range of results from attending the Institute. One team said that the institute was "Great help! Our team wrote its proposal for a faculty/staff learning community on the first-year experience" at the institute. Another team "relied heavily on the materials we got from the workshop and the understanding of FLCs that we developed there. . . . One of the institute attendees is leading the learning community." A participant who tried three topic-based groups reported: "One was successful, but two were not. Mostly the issue there was I tried to have others facilitate the groups and attempted to keep myself out of the mix. Two failed due to the facilitator and one succeeded modestly (also due to the facilitator)." A participant who has established four cohort FLCs and two topic-based FLCs since 2001 reports that it has been very difficult because he has been unable to get release time for participants, and his facilitator work has been "on top" of his work as a dean. The three volunteers he has recruited to be facilitators find the work "overwhelming for them." His recommendation is "funding and release time." And those in the Indiana University Southeast program found that participation in the institute itself was one of the best ways for a new FLC program developer, director, or facilitator to learn the aspects, activities, components, and outcomes of FLCs.

Campus-Based Programs. Two institutions, seeking to rapidly build a strong FLC program on their campuses, designed and implemented programs to select and prepare their facilitators. One campus focused on the organic emergence of communities, and the other developed a capacity-building project. Indiana University Southeast (IUS) and Ohio University began their quest to develop FLCs without knowing the exact topics, the number they could support, or who would serve as the facilitators. During fall 2002, IUS identified topics and then based their teaching symposium on those topics. During the spring 2003 semester, they identified facilitators and looked toward beginning the program. The development and selection process for IUS FLCs was based on knowledge of the specific needs of campus faculty. Ohio University, developing its program in response to a grant-funded initiative through the Ohio Learning Network, employed a formal selection model, seeking applications from faculty interested in becoming facilitators of learning communities during the 2003–04 academic year. Ultimately, nine faculty members were chosen and themselves became part of a 2002–03 FLC designed to develop their roles as facilitators of their own communities in the future.

The differing approaches employed by the two institutions reflect their circumstances as well as their institutional cultures. Both programs proved successful for their respective institutions, and details of each are offered here to highlight some of the issues involved in preparing individuals to facilitate FLCs.

Indiana University Southeast (IUS). IUS is a small commuter campus of 6,700 students and 180 faculty members that draws its student body from the local region. Establishing community among faculty is as important as establishing a sense of community among students.

The organizational structure of the IUS FLC program is somewhat unusual. There is no FLC program director; there is a managing office, the Institute for Learning and Teaching Excellence (ILTE), a teaching and learning center. An organizational chart showing the FLC leadership would have the Office of Academic Affairs and the ILTE at the top, followed immediately by the facilitators of the individual FLCs. The rather compact nature of the leadership chart is representative of IUS's underlying approach to FLCs: cooperation and collaboration.

The process of initiating the FLCs began by making FLCs the theme of IUS's annual teaching symposium. The 2003 teaching symposium marked the introduction of FLCs to IUS. Milton D. Cox from Miami University served as our keynote speaker and also offered a follow-up workshop for faculty interested in participating in FLCs. At the symposium, faculty members were asked to indicate their interest in participating in an FLC by signing up for one of the topics. The facilitator selection process was twofold. The first part was finding faculty who were willing to facilitate the teaching symposium small-group sessions, and the second part was identifying faculty who were willing to facilitate the FLCs.

During the first phase, the symposium planning committee identified FLCs as a theme and decided that it was most appropriate to base the first communities on the newly created IUS general education goals. Finding facilitators for symposium small-group sessions proved more difficult than selecting the topics. The key to identifying potential facilitators was familiarity with faculty and with their teaching and research interests. It was made clear to the symposium facilitators that leading a small-group session at the symposium entailed no other commitment. Small-group facilitators did not need to be experts on the topics or commit to facilitating an FLC. Interestingly, only two of the facilitators at the teaching symposium did not become facilitators of an FLC (although both opted to participate in FLCs where the facilitators were already in place).

At the conclusion of the symposium and again via an all-campus mailing and a faculty luncheon, faculty members were given the opportunity to select an FLC to join and to indicate interest in facilitating a group. Over sixty faculty members chose to participate in an FLC, and a large percentage of them indicated that they would be willing to facilitate an FLC.

The second phase of establishing the facilitators and membership of the FLCs began after reviewing the feedback from the symposium and the FLC membership forms. The FLCs were designed to be a collaborative process, so faculty members were first assigned to their preferred FLCs, and then the facilitator(s) was selected from those names.

The project committee, composed of the associate vice chancellor for academic affairs, the ILTE director, and the ILTE instructional designer, first met as a group to discuss FLC goals, obstacles, desired outcomes, and logistical issues. They then evaluated the FLC lists, discussed potential facilitators, and personally contacted each of them to provide more details about facilitator responsibilities and to confirm their willingness to serve. In some cases, the decision to have cofacilitators was made by the project committee in an effort to better support junior faculty facilitators; in other cases, it was done at the request of the faculty members.

To help create a community among the facilitators, the project committee met for lunch with all of the facilitators. During this initial meeting, the facilitators were given a copy of the *Faculty Learning Community Program Director's and Facilitator's Handbook* (Cox, 2003) and told about the 2003 International Faculty Learning Communities Conference and the New Developer's Institute: Designing, Implementing, and Leading FLCs, which were both to be held in June 2003. The facilitators were invited to attend one or both of the conferences. Five chose to attend the conference; three stayed for the New Developer's Institute, and they were joined by a member of the project committee. Offering the opportunity for the FLC facilitators to attend the conference together was the most important decision the project committee made. Not only did the group make meaningful connections with others working with FLCs, but they also developed stronger bonds with one another.

In an effort to ensure that the FLCs were adequately supported, the ILTE's instructional designer became an informal FLC program director, working with the facilitators; managing logistical and support issues; identifying conference, presentation, and publication opportunities; working to identify resources and best practices to share with FLCs; and serving as a liaison to the associate vice chancellor and ILTE director. Because the total funding for all seven FLCs is equivalent to what many universities are able to provide for one FLC, it was important to ensure that the facilitators did not feel overburdened. With one exception, none of the FLC facilitators receives any release time or additional compensation for serving as a facilitator. One facilitator receives release time because the FLC was part of a program that existed in a different form before becoming an FLC.

The development of the leadership for the FLCs included some key elements that led to long-term success for our FLC initiative. These elements form the basis of the following recommendations. First, involve the faculty as early and as often as possible. Second, provide a limited, rather easy jumping-off point in order to gauge interest not only in the idea of having FLCs but also in the topics to be offered. Third, establish a tentative FLC template that provides some control but remains flexible enough to allow individual FLCs and facilitators to take ownership of the program. Fourth, identify and make clear the support mechanism in place to work alongside (and on behalf of) the FLCs. Fifth, develop meaningful relationships between the program director and the facilitators, among the facilitators, and among the FLC members themselves. Sixth, in order to create ongoing community, encourage presentation and publication of FLC findings as well as attendance at conferences.

Ohio University. Ohio University is a large residential institution of 17,000 students that draws students from across the United States and several foreign countries. Many of the activities found at large universities help create a sense of community among both faculty and students. At the same time, the sheer size of such an institution leads to a decentralized workplace, with a myriad of challenges to organic emergence of cross-disciplinary community. As Ohio University embarks upon several major initiatives, FLCs provide a vehicle for ensuring deep and sustained culture change. As a means for disseminating new ideas and shared experiences, FLCs have an exponential effect—participants emerge as institutional leaders who in turn champion new ideas as essential to a viable institutional identity. Ohio University focused on capacity building, recognizing the importance of self-sustaining faculty learning communities for the future of the institution, and thus was able to begin the process of building their FLC program with an FLC for FLC facilitators.

A team of faculty and administrators, brought together in response to a grant initiative sponsored by the Ohio Learning Network (OLN), settled on a capacity-building project to quick-start a self-sustaining FLC program on campus. Two members of the team, directors of two of the faculty development centers on campus, simultaneously served as project directors and as facilitators of an FLC on faculty learning communities, in which all nine of the facilitators-to-be took part. This experiential model for faculty helped them explore the role of the FLC facilitator by understanding the dynamics of participating in an FLC. The project directors worked behind the scenes to develop the infrastructure to support a series of FLCs, meeting with deans and other administrators to secure their support, locating budget resources, and developing networks for communicating with the campus about the project. As learning community facilitators, the directors employed a constructivist approach, providing the scaffolding for faculty facilitators-to-be as they developed their understanding and articulation of their individual FLCs.

The FLC used many of the components associated with such communities and described in Cox's work (Cox, 2001), including social events (an opening dinner with spouses and partners at which the provost spoke, signifying the importance of the project to the institution, and a concluding celebratory breakfast, with the provost again in attendance), a retreat (the first formal meeting of the community, with Milt Cox as keynote speaker), and a project on the scholarship of teaching (creation of an original online case that was published electronically on the OLN Web site). In meetings over a five-month period, the FLC members addressed the following topics involved in developing an FLC: (1) clarifying goals and outcomes, (2) the FLC model and, specifically, linking goals and outcomes to FLC design, (3) models of academic community, (4) developing community-building exercises, (5) planning down to the precise details, (6) assessing and evaluating FLC goals and outcomes, and (7) sustaining FLCs on campus over time. Meeting biweekly, the FLC alternated between the scholarly project (creation of the online case) and the study of FLC development. Their time together increasingly reflected the needs and interest of the community members as they began to take ownership of the community.

To assist the facilitators in their planning work, the directors designed a number of tools, including an FLC goals inventory (Appendix A) that was modeled on the Teaching Goals Inventory (Angelo and Cross, 1993) and that provided the facilitators-in-training with an opportunity to consider the major outcomes that they hoped for from their community; a comprehensive planning inventory (Appendix B); and an exercise designed to assist in creating both a call for participants and a process for selecting from among applicants. Using classroom assessment techniques (Angelo and Cross, 1993), the group carefully considered successful models for leading and developing learning communities.

Both before and after their mutual study of community building and facilitation, FLC members were assessed regarding their perception of the hurdles they would face in successfully leading their community. Initially, they identified time issues (planning), overcoming negative attitudes, developing buy-in from faculty and administrators, logistics of scheduling and planning, and learning how to become a facilitator. After their work in the FLC, their new concerns once again listed time issues but had moved on to greater consideration of the logistics of the task ahead, including questions about funding (although provided with a small budget, they had begun to imagine further possibilities that would require an expanded budget), recruiting faculty participants, and scheduling activities and coordinating other aspects of the group.

Facilitators-to-be were also asked about the aspects of FLCs with which they were most and least familiar. At the beginning, they were most familiar with the logistics of getting a community under way and the enthusiasm needed to engage with their colleagues successfully. This changed by the end to familiarity with planning strategies for developing successful FLCs, how they would develop the content area of their individual FLCs, resources needed to create and sustain FLCs, and management of a successful FLC. In regard to their greatest questions about FLCs, initially, the most common response was simply "everything," followed by some of the specifics involved in setting up and managing an FLC. As they prepared to begin their own FLCs, their remaining questions and concerns centered on budgeting, dealing with group dynamics, and "making it all work." The project directors concluded that the FLC facilitators were ready to tackle their own groups but knew that a certain amount of a facilitator's training would come on the job.

Conclusion

Examination of the differences in approaches for establishing FLCs and developing the facilitators at IUS and Ohio University shows markedly different styles in both start-up and administration. The differences can be attributed to the differences between the two universities and the FLC classifications for each program. IUS chose a process of on-the-job training for all of the FLCs and their facilitators, while Ohio University opted to first work through the FLC process with their FLC facilitators. While both approaches have their advantages and disadvantages, each has been successful for its campus. In every case, the starting point for program development should address the desired outcomes and the local institutional culture.

Appendix A: Goals Inventory for Faculty Learning Community

Goals Inventory for Faculty Learning Community

Instructions: Read through each statement and circle the number that best corresponds to the degree of importance in relation to the outcomes you would like to achieve—for yourself and the other participants—through your faculty learning community next year.

1 = Not very important
2 = Not important
3 = Neither important nor unimportant
4 = Important
5 = Very important

1. Develop a perspective on teaching, learning, and other aspects of higher education beyond the perspective of your individual discipline
   1   2   3   4   5
2. Heighten appreciation of scholarly teaching and the scholarship of teaching
   1   2   3   4   5
3. Increase reflection on and about teaching
   1   2   3   4   5
4. Increase inspiration about teaching and scholarship
   1   2   3   4   5
5. Broaden view of teaching as an intellectual pursuit
   1   2   3   4   5
6. Learn more about the specific topic around which your learning community will be built   1   2   3   4   5
7. Increase understanding and awareness on campus about the specific topic of your learning community   1   2   3   4   5
8. Develop new course modules about the specific content of your learning community   1   2   3   4   5
9. Increase student achievement in relation to the specific focus of your learning community   1   2   3   4   5
10. Learn more about how your specific topic may influence and enhance teaching and learning   1   2   3   4   5
11. Increase comfort in your role as a member of the faculty
    1   2   3   4   5
12. Heighten awareness and understanding of the role of a faculty member at your institution   1   2   3   4   5
13. Develop a community of colleagues who continue as an informal support system after this FLC project ends   1   2   3   4   5
14. Develop a sense of community with colleagues around specific teaching projects that you carry out   1   2   3   4   5
15. Experience revitalization as a faculty member at Ohio University
    1   2   3   4   5
16. Successfully develop new/more learning objectives for your course
    1   2   3   4   5
17. Increase your general enthusiasm about teaching and learning
    1   2   3   4   5
18. Increase total effectiveness as a faculty member
    1   2   3   4   5

19. Increase technical skill as a teacher
    1   2   3   4   5
20. Increase comfort with and confidence in your teaching
    1   2   3   4   5
21. Increase understanding of and interest in the scholarship of teaching
    1   2   3   4   5
22. Heighten awareness of ways to integrate the teaching and research experiences
    1   2   3   4   5
23. Develop research and scholarly interests with respect to your discipline
    1   2   3   4   5
24. Produce a scholarly article or paper on teaching through your work in the community   1   2   3   4   5
25. Learn more about student achievement through scholarly research on teaching and learning   1   2   3   4   5

Instructions: Rank-order the following five foci for your learning community in order of importance from 1 to 5, where 1 = least important and 5 = most important. (Be sure to rank all five!)
_____Thinking about teaching beyond the classroom—in its broadest implications
_____Learning more about a specific pedagogical tool or strategy
_____Colleagueship and learning from others
_____Developing increased individual teaching skill and ability
_____Carrying out a teaching project and sharing it with the scholarly community
Once you have completed the inventory, please proceed to the next page to tally and interpret the results.

Interpretation of Results
For the first set of twenty-five items, add up the total score for each group of five as indicated below, then count the number of scores of "5" you recorded for each of those groups of items. (For example, if you circled a "3" for number 1, a "2" for number 2 and "5" on numbers 3–5, your total score would be 20 and the number of "5" scores circled would be 3.)

Items 1–5
Total score:_____
Number of 5s:_____
Items 6–10
Total score:_____
Number of 5s:_____
Items 11–15
Total score:_____
Number of 5s:_____
Items 16–20
Total score:_____
Number of 5s:_____
Items 21–25
Total score:_____
Number of 5s:_____

Now compare the group(s) of items in which you had both the highest score(s) and the most 5s with the final five items that you rank-ordered, which are in the same order as the first twenty-five items. (Thus, if your highest score was on items 1–5, you probably should have ranked "thinking about teaching beyond the classroom" first.) The key for the groups of items is as follows:

• The first group of five items focuses on an intellectual approach to or discussion about teaching as the major goal of the work you undertake with your learning community.

• The second group of five items focuses on gaining specific topical information regarding the focus for your learning community (for example, learning more about technological applications to effect learning outcomes) as the major goal for your community.

• The third group of five items focuses on developing a sense of connection to others and to the institution as the major goal of your community.

• The fourth group of five items focuses on enhancing general teaching effectiveness as the major goal of your community.

• The final five items focus on the scholarship of teaching and teaching projects or research as the major goal of your community.

Appendix B: Planning Inventory for Faculty Learning Community

Planning Inventory for Faculty Learning Community

Name of community:
Facilitator:
Community focus (2–3 sentence description):

Part I: Participants
Anticipated size of community:
FLC members (for example, faculty, student associates, consultants; targeted departments or subject areas; include all that apply):
Plan for recruiting members (steps taken, channels used to publicize, and time line):
Application process (What will you ask potential participants to submit as an application, and how will you make decisions about selecting from among potential applicants? If you have already worked on this, you may want to attach an application form and then describe your criteria for selection):
Plan for involving student associates or consultants (if applicable):

Part II: Curriculum
Focus book:
Topics you plan on preparing (others may be added as the group begins working, but what will you plan on starting out with?):
Role of consultants or student associates (if applicable) in facilitating this curriculum:

Part III: Logistics
How will you communicate with FLC members?
What is your plan if schedules don't mesh?
What are expectations for members' participation, and how will you communicate these?

Part IV: Scholarship of Teaching
What kinds of teaching projects do you anticipate being carried out by FLC members? And will you expect or ask them to choose a focus course and share it with the group?
What kinds of support will you provide to your FLC members as they design their teaching projects?

What goals or expectations do you have for sharing the results of the scholarship of teaching?

Part V: Budget

You have a total of $200 available to spend on your group, and you can request up to an additional $200. Please list your anticipated costs below, and include any additional financial sources you hope to tap. Note that we may be able to do some bulk buying on focus books, thus reducing the cost for all. Include everything you would need in the list below, but please place an asterisk by the items that are your highest priority and for which you will use the monies indicated above. Although we cannot promise additional funding, we will seek sources for it; thus, it will be useful to see what you would use.

Amount budgeted per participant (divide total by anticipated number of participants):

Part VI: Assessment

What are your initial thoughts on ways to assess whether you are achieving the goals of your learning community? Note that we will discuss this further at a future meeting.

References

Angelo, T. A., and Cross, K. P. *Classroom Assessment Techniques: A Handbook for College Teachers.* (2nd ed.) San Francisco: Jossey-Bass, 1993.

Cox, M. D. "Faculty Learning Communities: Change Agents for Transforming Institutions into Learning Organizations." *To Improve the Academy,* 2001, *19,* 69–93.

Cox, M. D. *Faculty Learning Community Program Director's and Facilitator's Handbook.* Oxford, Ohio: Miami University, 2003.

Kalish, A., Harper, K. A., and Woodard, R. D. "The 'Accidental' Faculty Learning Community." Paper presented at the 1st annual International Faculty Learning Community Conference, Pomona, Calif., June 2003.

KARIN L. SANDELL *is founding director of the Center for Teaching Excellence at Ohio University and recently served as a Fulbright Senior Specialist, providing workshops and seminars on faculty development in Namibia.*

KATY WIGLEY *is an instructional design and technology specialist in the Institute for Learning and Teaching Excellence at Indiana University Southeast, where she coordinates the faculty learning community initiative and cofacilitates the Service-Learning FLC.*

ANN KOVALCHICK *is founding director of the Center for Innovations in Technology for Learning at Ohio University.*

Previous FLC facilitators share experiences and insights about group process and provide their advice for facilitating successful communities.

Facilitating Faculty Learning Communities: A Compact Guide to Creating Change and Inspiring Community

Martha C. Petrone, Leslie Ortquist-Ahrens

> "Would you please tell me which way I have to go from here?"
>
> "That depends a good deal on where you want to get to."
> —Lewis Carroll, *Alice's Adventures in Wonderland*

As the faculty learning community (FLC) model becomes an integral part of faculty development efforts at more and more colleges and universities, faculty developers with little or no previous FLC experience find themselves in the role of FLC facilitator. Just as FLCs address a range of ever-changing factors affecting the teaching and learning environment, FLC facilitators assume different roles as they guide their community members toward their individual and collective outcomes.

What does it take to be an effective FLC facilitator? When a working group at the 2003 Summer Institute for New Faculty Learning Community Developers reported the results of their discussion on what it takes to be an effective FLC facilitator, even those with extensive experience in leading FLCs listened with rapt attention. As FLC facilitators, many had not really considered which direction they should go, where they wanted to get to, or potential pitfalls they might confront along the way.

In this chapter, two of the participants in that discussion—a faculty development professional charged with initiating a new FLC program at a small liberal arts college and an experienced FLC facilitator from a medium-size, research-intensive university—recreate that dialogue to provide an understanding of group process and suggest a range of important questions that facilitators can consider in advance in order to contribute to overall success for their FLCs. Although there is a wealth of literature on group dynamics and leading groups, in order to provide narrative coherence, we tell our story independent of such references. Those interested in the literature can consult Wenger, McDermott, and Snyder (2002).

Why do you use the term "facilitator" rather than "leader"? Although unique in their structure and desired outcomes, FLCs require the same team-building guidance as any other work group. In the course of a semester or academic year, the FLC facilitator will function in a nonlinear way in three main roles—*champion, coordinator,* and *energizer.* However, unlike the goal of a traditional group leader, the ultimate goal of a facilitator is not to maintain the leadership position but to help move the members of the FLC to the point where they gradually assume these three roles themselves.

That seems very different from the leadership model with which most faculty are familiar. Can you explain how it is different? To understand the facilitation needs of an FLC, we can look at some fundamentals of group dynamics. The success of any group is measured along three dimensions: *outcomes,* the actual results; *tasks,* the efficiency, effectiveness, clarity, and adaptability of the process for achieving those outcomes; and *relationships,* the level of mutual respect, trust, support, and cooperation group members experience as they work together to accomplish the outcomes.

FLCs can present a challenge for the facilitator because one of the desired outcomes is in fact the relationship dimension—often more so than is the case in the typical classroom. In addition to providing a vehicle for enhancing student learning through application of insights from findings of individual or group projects to classroom practice and work with students, FLCs also are designed to engender a sense of community within and beyond individual groups and to foster collegiality across disciplines and units. While the relationship dimension is an important part of classroom teaching, facilitators may find it to be an even more prominent issue in the FLC context. An effective FLC facilitator strives to balance the task and relationship dimensions of the group process while motivating change and high-quality outcomes.

It sounds like facilitating an FLC is like chasing a moving target. Milton Cox tells of his experiences in facilitating the Alumni Teaching Scholars Faculty Learning Community in its early years at Miami University. The inaugural year of the program went smoothly; the FLC had shared goals, well-delineated plans, and tangible teaching and learning and community outcomes. Not unlike most of us after we teach a course successfully for the first time, Milt had a sense of clarity and confidence about how to lead the second year's group through the FLC process—that is, until they actually met. With different personalities, disciplinary perspectives, cultural backgrounds, learning styles, and goals, the participants did not fit well into the mold that Milt had developed in the first year. He said it was then that he learned to incorporate key components from year to year but to leave space in the process for the participants to determine both their individual and collective outcomes and the ways they would achieve them.

Through careful balancing of roles, a facilitator can create a space for work to take place and for community to grow. As noted earlier, FLC facilitators have three main operational roles that interrelate and overlap. They generally correspond to the dimensions of group dynamics, with the champion connected to outcomes, the coordinator overseeing the tasks, and the energizer encouraging relationships. The facilitator will move fluidly in and out of the three roles as necessary throughout the life of the FLC and even during the course of a single meeting. The predominant role at any particular time is based in great measure on how and to what extent the facilitator will be involved in directing the FLC. A closer look at each role will help to clarify what is involved for the facilitator.

What is a champion? FLCs are vehicles for institutional, educational, and personal change. By keeping members' focus on the big picture while motivating participants to take the risk to change in their individual arenas, the champion serves as a catalyst for academic change. Change can be uncomfortable. Generally, people will risk change only when they expect that it will result in some personal gains, believe that the change makes sense, think that it is the right thing to do, believe it is the right time for a change, or respect the person who is championing the change. The champion provides and nurtures that motivation by helping FLC members negotiate change and overcome barriers.

In this role, the facilitator is engaged in the content of the FLC, providing resources, information, and insights. Specifically, a champion would be likely to provide access to leading articles and other resources, in order to provide a knowledge base for the participants, and encourage participants to find and share high-quality resources, including those on loosely related topics. In the role of champion, the facilitator creates a nonthreatening, yet challenging climate that will encourage participants to move outside their comfort zone; encourages adaptation to new approaches and expanding skills; instills confidence in the FLC process; and encourages innovation while remaining mindful of environmental constraints. The champion is also a vocal advocate for the FLC program, communicating achievements and advancing the overall goals of the FLC program throughout the institution. With a broad knowledge of university politics, policies, and procedures, the facilitator as champion may even be able to provide opportunities to initiate broader departmental and institutional change.

What is a coordinator? The coordinator focuses on the operational and logistical aspects of the learning community. In this role, the facilitator uses organizational and management skills to advance the purpose and objectives of the FLC. In addition to creating a framework to guide the FLC's work, the coordinator oversees day-to-day tasks and responsibilities.

As coordinator, the facilitator may handle many of the arrangements and much of the planning in the early weeks of the FLC. As time passes, through delegation or by fostering volunteerism, the coordinator can enlist members' help with the range of duties involved in the smooth operation of the group. Initial tasks of a coordinator would be to identify the key components of the FLC in consultation with the FLC program director and build a framework for the semester or year around the key components and the FLC objectives. To ensure smooth functioning of the FLC, the coordinator may make or delegate arrangements for meetings, retreats, seminars, conferences, or meals; order shared readings; manage scheduling to ensure maximum attendance at events; determine methods for disseminating information to community members; and coordinate resource collection and dissemination. The coordinator plans meeting agendas to balance individual work with collaborative engagement and facilitates discussions. In addition, the coordinator maintains documentation and records and communicates well and frequently with the person overseeing the program.

What exactly is an energizer? Just as faculty members monitor and sometimes orchestrate classroom interactions, the energizer monitors and directs the interaction of FLC members, with the goal of encouraging participation, involvement, and mutual engagement. In this capacity, the facilitator refrains from getting engaged in the deliberations and decision making of the FLC. By thoughtfully observing and providing feedback on both the focus and the harmony of the group, the energizer makes any necessary interventions to bring the group back to the overarching goals of the FLC program: to enhance student learning and to build community and foster relationships across disciplines. Specific tasks of the energizer include facilitating the creation of shared goals and ground rules at an early meeting; facilitating the establishment of mechanisms for shared decisions making; and helping to forge connections among participants to motivate them to work toward and achieve outcomes. The energizer encourages humor and enjoyment; nurtures a climate of mutual respect and trust with the ultimate goal of allowing each person's voice to be heard; and models effective interpersonal communication behaviors such as listening actively, asking clarifying questions, waiting for those who take longer to respond, summarizing, empathizing, and seeking consensus. The energizer may facilitate conflict resolution when necessary and provide feedback when the group focus wanders or harmony dissolves.

Are there particular qualities or qualifications that are absolutely essential in a facilitator of FLCs? As you have no doubt figured out by now, there is not just one profile of an ideal facilitator, nor are there any hard and fast rules that dictate what ensures success. Strong facilitators vary in their individual preferences and styles. At the same time, there are some general qualities, skills, and prior experiences that help an individual contribute to the development of cohesive and productive communities. Key qualities and attitudes include flexibility, tolerance for ambiguity, mindfulness, creativity in thinking, enthusiasm about learning, respect for human diversity, an abiding interest in the FLC topic, and openness to innovation and new ideas. A successful facilitator is likely to bring to the table good organizational skills, excellent interpersonal skills, an ability and willingness to motivate others, savvy about institutional politics, the ability to initiate and sustain dialogue and to include—or at least to invite—all voices, and at least some knowledge of small group dynamics. Ideally, the facilitator will also have had some prior experience with communal learning.

At first glance, the preceding list may seem daunting. Yet on closer examination, these qualities, attitudes, and experiences are familiar to many faculty members—at least intuitively—and are the very ones they call upon daily in the classroom and in collegial relationships. Therefore, FLC facilitators can draw on their teaching experiences and abilities to manage the agenda, create community, promote change, encourage learning, negotiate and locate resources, and communicate effectively.

Are there any qualities in the lists above that are more important than others? One of the most important qualities is flexibility. It allows the facilitator to move smoothly from one role to another and back again, encouraging members' broader engagement and greater productivity as well as allowing for serendipitous happenings. As Jack Gifford, one of the FLC facilitators at Miami University, says,

> Stay flexible! Nothing happens as fast as you think it will. Be willing to pause, take valuable side trips dictated by the ebb and flow of the group. Don't push too hard and listen a lot more than you talk. Good things will happen, but it takes time and will not follow the road map drawn on day one. Also, be sure that everyone is having fun and enjoying the process. Do fun things. Eat well. Build a culture of trust and mutual respect. Learn from the diversity and creativity of the individuals in the group. [Cox, 2004]

Mindfulness is also fundamental to a facilitator's success. The FLC represents a blending of disciplinary cultures and diverse perspectives. As academics, we are often accustomed to being experts in our field and engaging with others who share our knowledge. In an FLC, there is a wide range of knowledge about a variety of different topics. Being mindful of the rich resources that members bring will help a facilitator draw out insights and promote creative solutions. In addition, new facilitators should be encouraged to make an informal self-inventory of their strengths in the areas mentioned earlier, as well as their opportunities for growth. By doing so mindfully before setting out, they will be more likely to anticipate areas of challenge, learn new skills where necessary, and acknowledge and accept any discomfort or insecurity they may experience as they engage in the process.

What are potential pitfalls for the FLC facilitator to avoid? To be optimally successful, it is important not only that FLCs be clearly structured experiences that occur with some regularity but also that members have opportunities and be given latitude to pursue areas of interest that may sometimes seem tangential. In addition, facilitators must be able to react spontaneously within the general structures set out by the program and agreed upon by each individual community.

The first set of pitfalls a facilitator should be aware of have to do with reading the environment and making necessary adjustments. If he or she is impatient with the unfolding process, a facilitator may respond with too much structure, be overly directive or too didactic, and squelch creativity. On the other end of the spectrum, a facilitator may provide too little structure, failing to clarify and periodically revisit expectations and goals for projects or other outcomes, to establish guidelines or ground rules for the group, or to engage in necessary team building and promotion of positive group processes.

Beyond these two major tendencies, facilitators should be wary of other pitfalls. Facilitators can face difficulties if they are unable to tolerate ambiguity; if they fail to intervene when a participant hijacks the agenda or derails the process; or if they fail (on the other hand) to allow for flexibility and exploration of apparently tangential topics of great interest to the group. Other pitfalls that facilitators should avoid include failing to encourage all voices to be heard (that is, failing to draw out or actively engage quieter or more introverted participants) and allowing individuals to approach them outside the group rather than working through complaints or conflicts involving other group members *within* the group. Facilitators should try not to second-guess themselves constantly in their role as facilitators, failing to trust the process. Facilitators may also have problems if they lose connection with the overarching goals for the learning community program and with the guidelines established by the group or if they fail to determine when it is more important to engage with the content (the topic of the FLC) or model the process (demonstrate support for each participant's goals). Such problems can be avoided through careful selection methods and preparation programs, such as those described in Chapter Four.

Any final thoughts? FLCs provide a collaborative arena in which colleagues have the time and opportunity to reflect on their teaching, their discipline, their institution, and themselves. By creating a safe environment for the honest engagement of ideas and feelings, the FLC facilitator helps to move the faculty outside of their disciplinary comfort zones and into the realm of intellectual and interpersonal connections. Through this process, teaching and learning are meaningfully enhanced and often transformed. There is no doubt that being an FLC facilitator can be challenging. By supporting colleagues through fostering change, encouraging innovation, and inspiring community, the facilitator can have a profound impact not only on student learning but also on the quality of faculty members' shared work environment.

References

Cox, M. D. *Faculty Learning Community Program Director's and Facilitator's Handbook.* Oxford, Ohio: Miami University, 2004.

Wenger, E., McDermott, R., and Snyder, W. M. *A Guide to Managing Knowledge: Cultivating Communities of Practice.* Boston: Harvard Business School Press, 2002.

MARTHA C. PETRONE *is coordinator of humanities and fine arts at Miami University–Middletown in Middletown, Ohio. She has served as a consultant to the Faculty Learning Community on U.S. Cultures Course Development and as cofacilitator for the Faculty Learning Community on Using Difference in Teaching and Learning at the Oxford and regional campuses.*

LESLIE ORTQUIST-AHRENS *is director of the Center for Teaching and Learning at Otterbein College in Westerville, Ohio, where she currently facilitates a learning community for junior faculty and oversees a new professional learning community program generously supported by the McGregor Fund.*

A small state agency used the FLC model to collaborate with campuses on faculty development efforts that resulted in successful implementation of pedagogically robust and technologically enhanced programs.

Developing a Statewide Faculty Learning Community Program

Sheryl Hansen, Alan Kalish, Wayne E. Hall, Catherine M. Gynn, Mary Louise Holly, Dan Madigan

In the spring of 2002, inspired by ambitious goals and a constrained time-line, members of the Ohio Learning Network (OLN) returned to a conversation that had begun two years earlier and that had centered on one primary question: How could a young state agency best collaborate with campuses on faculty development efforts that would result in pedagogically robust and technologically enhanced programs, courses, modules, and learning objects such as videos and Web sites? Their answer: faculty learning communities.

The Ohio Learning Network

OLN was created in 1999, based on recommendations in the *Technology in the Learning Communities of Tomorrow* report that described "how Ohio's schools, colleges, and universities can become interconnected learning communities through new methods, new relationships, and new technologies" (Ohio Technology in Education Steering Committee, 1996, front cover). Funded by the Ohio Board of Regents, OLN is designed to infuse new technologies into established courses and programs at Ohio colleges and universities.

Ohio has a rich history of learning community activity, support, knowledge, and experience, including Milt Cox's pioneering of faculty learning communities (FLCs) at Miami University. The Ohio Board of Regents had

NEW DIRECTIONS FOR TEACHING AND LEARNING, no. 97, Spring 2004 © Wiley Periodicals, Inc.

previously supported the development of the Ohio Teaching Enhancement Program (OTEP), building on successes of FLCs for early-career faculty (Cox and Jeep, 2000).

Developing Technology-Enhanced Programs

With many of the same people involved with both OTEP and OLN, we at the OLN had a unique platform for statewide faculty development programs that made conditions ripe for scaling up participation in FLCs.

The Learning Communities Initiative. The 2002 call for proposals stated, "The initiative provides the opportunity to develop and support communities that are learning to use technology, to bring together the best of what we know about how people learn, the best of what we know about exciting technology resources, with the best of what we can do with our collective talents, commitment, and goals for education" (Ohio Learning Network, 2002). The products and the processes sought by this initiative were planned to go beyond individual members and institutions, and what we would learn about community engagement would inform not only immediate participants but also students, colleagues, other institutions, and other states. The OLN team designed the OLN Learning Communities Initiative to engage faculty participants in a series of activities and experiences to maximize the likelihood of success, both in terms of projects and in terms of building FLCs. This required a clear statement of goals, a two-phase application process, and a framework and structure that would provide a foundation from which each FLC could build and sustain its work.

Goals. The goals of the OLN Initiative called for each FLC to work together to learn and apply and share knowledge about the following items: innovations in teaching, learning, and technology; collaboration and cooperation among members of the FLC, among all faculty, and among students; reflective practice—participants' and others'; problem-based learning; the process of creating, using, and sharing digital resources; assessment of the projects and processes of community development in order to learn from our experiences; and the ways in which technology can support these goals. The complete request for proposals and program description is available on the OLN Web site at http://www.oln.org.

Selection. The first phase of the application process asked principal investigators from each institution to define a project, recruit a team (or identify an existing one), and demonstrate institutional support. FLCs selected for a readiness grant were given $3,000 and three months to develop their final project plan, including an expanded description of goals, expected outcomes and deliverables, a timeline, and assessment methods. The final project plan was the major component of an implementation grant proposal.

FLCs that successfully completed the readiness phase could apply for $25,000 implementation grants. These grants were designed to help FLCs enrich faculty knowledge; build expertise; and produce portable, scalable, and digital learning resources for Ohio institutions. Both phases of this process were predicated on a collaborative work process that built community among participants.

Each FLC was to consist of eight to twelve members. OLN expected each community to include a variety of members representing a broad range of roles, expertise, experiences, and learning styles. Thus, FLCs could include faculty, staff, librarians, instructional designers, students, teachers, and community members.

OLN sought communities whose work and membership spanned traditional disciplinary "silos" and boundaries while focusing on the core mission of OLN: using technologies to support student learning. Each proposal was reviewed for evidence of engagement, alignment with campus policy, assessment components, collaborative processes, public access, and the delivery of digital resources. The selection process was more developmental than competitive. We looked for projects for which additional state resources could maximize sustainability and extend, speed up, or deepen project work. As a result of the selection process, twenty-three Ohio institutions received implementation grants as principal investigators for thirty-one FLCs. Overall thirty-two institutions were included as partners within those communities. (See Appendix A for a list of the selected FLCs.)

Framework. Drawing on the best knowledge available about how people learn and about cultural change, the conceptual, methodological, and structural frameworks that support the Learning Communities Initiative were intentionally developmental and intended to be transformative. While tinkering around the edges may produce change in individual classrooms, the kind of transformation in educational settings that enables students to engage in a continual process of learning is not likely to take place without concomitant changes in the larger culture. It was this kind of transformation that we sought to help to ignite and sustain. *Doing* things differently, while important, would not alone work for very long; the initiative had to be catalytic. Thus, OLN needed to offer structural elements that could sustain the momentum that sparked the initiative in the first place.

Consistent with continual development and being catalytic, three key ingredients provided a methodological foundation for the OLN initiative:

Academic Quality Improvement Program. Eleven Ohio institutions are members of the Academic Quality Improvement Program (AQIP), a national organization with a hundred institutional members. Launched in July 1999 with a grant from the Pew Charitable Trusts, AQIP infuses the principles and benefits of continuous improvement into the culture of colleges and universities by providing an alternative process through which an already-accredited institution can maintain its accreditation from the Higher Learning Commission. With AQIP, an institution demonstrates that it meets accreditation standards and expectations through sequences of events that align with the ongoing activities that characterize organizations striving to improve their performance.

AQIP's accreditation and evaluation criteria and the Learning Community Initiative's assessment processes are philosophically compatible. The initiative's projects and activities can provide rich and representative evidence (required by AQIP) in addressing Core Components. Typical FLC activities significantly address four AQIP criteria: Student Learning and Effective Teaching; Acquisition, Discovery, and Application of Knowledge; Preparing for the Future; and Engagement and Service.

Action Research. Action research enables researchers to improve their practice as they "pursue action (or change) and research (or understanding) at the same time. . . . In most of its forms it does this by using a cyclic or spiral process which alternates between action and critical reflection and in the later cycles, continuously refining methods, data and interpretation in the light of the understanding developed in the earlier cycles. . . . In most of its forms it is also participative (among other reasons, change is usually easier to achieve when those affected by the change are involved) and qualitative" (Dick, 1999). The OLN assessment processes for the communities, Learning Institutes, and the Learning Community Initiative itself are built upon the reflective, questioning practices of action research. Through the discipline of setting collaborative goals and then systematically using reflective practice for continuous improvement, OLN is building the transformational outcomes they seek.

Case Studies. Often used in action research, case study reports offer an evolving database and a heuristic method for analysis, synthesis, and interpretation of experiences, enabling FLCs to learn from one another, as well as from their own experiences. Therefore, rather than requiring typical reporting processes or comprehensive case studies, OLN required the development of reflective writings for public review.

Starting. As the planning team discussed the initiative, we realized that the concept of an FLC would be new to many (perhaps most) of the grant recipients, for whom committee work would be the most common point of reference. It became apparent that we would need to pay particular attention to networking and building common ground, not only within the thirty-one individual learning communities but also within the larger statewide group. Therefore, the framework we devised provided assistance in creating communities and supporting the work of individual groups and the larger community.

The first OLN Initiative networking event was a one-day kickoff conference held centrally, in Columbus. All of the more than 250 members of the thirty-one FLCs were invited, and 196 attended. This event sought to provide communities with information about the initiative and its goals; about the concept of FLCs; and about the possibilities for using technologies to support reflective practice, community, and deep learning. As an off-campus event, it also provided many of the FLCs with an initial bonding experience.

Milton D. Cox, director of the Center for the Enhancement of Learning and Teaching at Miami University, provided a keynote discussion of FLCs. Van Weigel, professor of ethics and economic development at Eastern College, spoke about "Learning Communities and Knowledge Management: Preparing Students for the 21st Century Workplace." Small-group sessions were offered on a variety of topics related to the goals of the initiative. The complete schedule and video of the plenary sessions, as well as text and PowerPoint files for most of the presentations, are available on the OLN Web site at http://www.oln.org.

The Learning Communities and Institutes

There are twenty-three diverse institutions as principal investigators representing thirty-two different institutions (twenty-one public, eleven private) of higher education, plus their partners, represented within the thirty-one communities. There was a broad array of types of institutional support and faculty development. Partners included K–12 schools, Head Start, Hospice of the Western Reserve, United Way, a Vietnamese university, and an ecumenical consortium. The smallest student body was under two thousand, and the largest was over fifty thousand. FLC size ranged from six to seventeen members.

Five January 2003 learning institutes were one key to the success of the Learning Communities Initiative. Each institute was theme-related and provided members of five to seven FLCs with expertise, time to bond as a team, critiquing, networking, idea sharing, and reflection away from campus. The initiative's planning group intended for the January learning institutes to be offered regionally, with a common set of core activities and outcomes alongside more customized components to meet the needs of participating FLCs.

The themes of the five learning institutes were Collaborating, Improving Our Teaching, Preparing Future Teachers, Building and Assessing Sharable Content, and Supporting Student Learning; the themes were selected from the projects of the FLCs. The institutes were of roughly equal size, similar interests, and regional diversity. A second meeting, The Gathering, was held in June to develop our digital repository and host the critically important final high-tech sharing and celebration event.

Expertise from each institute member has been offered to other faculty members on that campus, partly for wider buy-in and partly for additional insights and ideas. Institute participants reported that they found their own views had been enlightened in responding to diverse ideas and challenges. Successful institute experiences were facilitated by holding early conversations among all five institute planners, carefully assessing participant needs, identifying able and willing mentors, planning appropriate facilities and activities, and respecting the diverse needs of the multiple FLCs.

What Are We Learning?

We learned many lessons from the implementation of the OLN FLCs.

The Unexpected. Of course, we experienced surprises along the way. We expected fifteen to twenty communities to respond to the request for proposals, but received forty-two proposals, thirty-one of which were particularly strong. The planning team rethought every aspect of the initiative in light of the large response and shifted into new structures. Very intentionally, we moved toward a developmental, less competitive overall philosophy. We shifted toward decentralized, less-mandated expectations and decision making and toward local and regional capacity building, with less top-down structure. Despite the many new challenges and old paradigms we bumped into, this was the right thing to do, and we will continue to work and plan in this way.

When the FLCs were formed, most facilitators had had no previous involvement in a learning community. This was a greater challenge than we expected. In addition, the norms of committee structures and the dogma of hierarchies (either being told what to do or telling others what to do) are powerful deterrents to community building. Strong support for facilitators is needed to address these obstacles.

Insights. This expansive initiative required tremendous time, energy, passion, collaboration, expertise, and political savvy. Flexibility was required of every person involved. Time, however, was the number one prerequisite for success in all aspects. If an initiative offers just money or the promise of "new pedagogical tricks" to faculty, it will not create sufficient sustainable buy-in for success. The most effective FLCs find ways to respect and work around the demanding time commitments, all the while engaging participants through a sense of community in a shared pedagogical vision.

We found that it is important for maintaining momentum and long-term success that the funded projects are authentic campus projects rather than new work created on top of other workloads. Declining institutional budgets could be supplemented by maximizing state and institutional resources. The state planning committee members' ethics informed us that we must *walk our talk* or else we—and the Initiative—would not enjoy the credibility we wanted, so we moved away from a competitive review/selection model toward a capacity-building, action research approach.

The sequencing and scaffolding provided by initiative events worked out well. Attendance at a two-day learning institute was perceived initially by many FLCs as an inconvenience, but eventually the institute experience was recognized as extremely useful for group cohesiveness, refocusing, and accomplishing goals.

We cannot overemphasize the importance of providing FLCs with a safe, supportive grant environment in which mistakes, detours, goal shifts, and failure, were expected. We often provided examples of mistakes, to promote and enable the sharing of challenges typically kept secret. In addition, the learning institutes provided additional opportunities for groups to collaborate, address challenges, and solve problems. We received considerable positive feedback from FLCs about their institutes.

Not surprisingly, an effective and passionate FLC facilitator is also central to FLC success. As discussed in Chapters Four and Five, selecting and preparing FLC facilitators should be carefully planned, and resources must be provided to give the facilitators enough time to meet the needs of the FLC.

The most effective, creative, and stable communities took advantage of two institutional factors that ultimately led to success: (1) an institutional commitment to the importance of faculty growth and development and (2) FLC goals that were clearly aligned with institutional goals.

A powerful factor working against collaboration is the influence of institutional reappointment, tenure, and promotion systems that reward solo and "silo" behavior (acting as isolated individuals or units). This was true across the variety of institutions that were involved in this initiative. Institutional and disciplinary expectations and standards must be rethought and overhauled in order for real transformational change to occur. We have begun to address these issues head-on and will increase attention to institutional, cross-institutional, and state policy development and support in our next request for proposals.

A shift from traditional grant reporting to a more formative process was essential. OLN needed evidence to show that the initiative had positively affected faculty learning and professional practice in Ohio; therefore, year one project deliverables were necessary. It was agreed that public sharing of the project outcomes and process knowledge would occur. Requiring both *Portraits of Practice: Case Records* (to meet the overall learning goals for participants) and the digital repository (for the public sharing of knowledge, processes, and learning objects) was effective in meeting our goals.

What's Next?

We are actively engaged in several continuing-the-momentum activities. A commitment to support FLCs remains a priority at OLN. It is also important to share the lessons learned and outcomes of the FLCs. We make the wealth of knowledge gained through the initiative widely available through the E-Learning Athenaeum of Ohio, OLN's e-learning repository; through Ohio-Learns!, Ohio's portal to distance learning opportunities; and through Web sites, news briefs, online communities, presentations, and articles.

Eleven of the thirty-one 2002–03 FLCs were awarded continuation grants for 2003–04 to continue the momentum and explore institutional policy challenges more directly. We also will offer two one-day learning institutes.

A new Learning Communities Initiative request for proposals has been issued for 2004–05 FLCs. We are cognizant of the shifting state budget environment, new demands for fiscal and outcomes accountability, and the need to develop authentic and viable metrics to better define the impact of the initiative. The insights of our planning team learning community, as well as FLCs from across the state, will guide us.

Appendix A: 2003–04 Ohio Learning Network Faculty Learning Communities

Belmont Technical College
 1. Faculty Team Teaching/Course Development in Information Services: Library Paraprofessional

Bluffton College
 2. Expanding the Learning Circle

Bowling Green State University
 3. Quality Assurance in the New Medium: Putting Graduate Courses in Educational Foundations On-Line
 4. Technical Literacy for Graduate Scholar-Teachers

Central State University
 5. The CSU Learning Communities Initiative

Columbus State Community College
 6. Alternative Associate Degree in Nursing

Cuyahoga Community College
 7. The Technology and Information Literacy Initiative Learning Community for First Year Experience Students—Developing a Dynamic Learning Environment

Franciscan University of Steubenville
 8. Bioethics and Ethics Studies of the Master of Theology by Distance Education

Hocking College
 9. Electronic Methods of Documenting Student Learning of Success Skills

Kent State University
 10. First Year Experience Learning Community
 11. Faculty and Future Faculty Learning Community
 12. Collaborative Technology for Students

Lorain County Community College
 13. Exploring Electronic Portfolios as a Form of Alternative Assessment

Miami University
 14. Learning Community: Technology and the Humanities

The Ohio State University
 15. Rich Media for Science and the Humanities
 16. Seminar on Interprofessional Care

Ohio University
 17. Ohio University Scholarly Communities of Practice in Education

Ohio University–Zanesville
18. Ohio University Regional Higher Education

Owens Community College
19. Best Practices in the Development of Web-Based Instruction

University of Akron
20. Mobile and Equitable Scientific Inquiry

University of Cincinnati
21. Early Childhood Education Virtual Resource Room Website
22. Building Emotional Intelligence via Student Learning Communities
23. Development of an On-line Instructional Tool: Learning Module on Social Responsibility

University of Dayton
24. Integrating Notebook Computing into the Higher Education Classroom
25. The Summer E-Learning Experience Collaborative Team (SELECT)

The University of Findlay
26. Digital Learning Models Alliance

University of Toledo
27. Technology Learning Community for Head Start Teachers: Technology Empowerment

Ursuline College
28. What You Want? Baby We Got It—Ursuline College and Hospice of the Western Reserve Learning Community

Wright State University
29. Learning for Teaching: How a Learning Community Engages in Curriculum Renewal

Youngstown State University
30. The Expansion of Criminal Justice Education: A Learning Community
31. Distance Learning in Introductory Programming Classes

References

Cox, M. D., and Jeep, J. M. "Taking Your Best Faculty Development Program Statewide in the 21st Century: Mentoring Other Campuses Regarding Junior Faculty." Paper presented at the 25th annual conference of the Professional and Organizational Development Network, Vancouver, Canada, Nov. 2000.

Dick, B. "What Is Action Research?" [http://www.scu.edu.au/schools/gcm/ar/whatisar.html]. 1999.

Ohio Learning Network. "Request for Proposals." [http://www.oln.org/funding/lcomm.php]. Mar. 2002, p. 1.

Ohio Technology in Education Steering Committee. *Technology in the Learning Communities of Tomorrow: Beginning the Transformation.* Columbus: State of Ohio, July 1996.

SHERYL HANSEN is director of professional development programs at the Ohio Learning Network.

ALAN KALISH is director of faculty and TA development at The Ohio State University.

WAYNE E. HALL is vice provost for faculty development at the University of Cincinnati.

CATHERINE M. GYNN is the technology enhanced learning and research coordinator at The Ohio State University.

MARY LOUISE HOLLY is director of the Faculty Professional Development Center at Kent State University.

DAN MADIGAN is director of the Center for Teaching, Learning and Technology at Bowling Green State University.

As FLC programs expand, there is an increasing need to use technology and diplomacy to manage the details of multiple concurrent FLCs.

Managing Multiple Faculty Learning Communities

Melody Ayn Barton, Laurie Richlin

As your faculty learning community (FLC) program grows from one to multiple FLCs, organization becomes both more complex and more important. It is essential to gather information early and efficiently while building rapport and a sense of community with each FLC member. Organizational structures and tools can help FLC program directors and their support staff to maintain an efficient and effective program.

Duties and Tasks

Managing multiple FLCs includes coordination, scheduling, budgeting and spending, and resource provision for each FLC and for FLC participants; scheduling and hosting a variety of events; and information gathering and management.

Schedule Coordination and Budget. As complicated as it is to coordinate the schedules of eight to ten members of one FLC group, it is much more difficult to work with additional FLCs. Figure 7.1 shows a calendar of FLC activities at Miami University for the first two weeks of April 2003. The calendar, created with the MeetingMaker program, shows meeting times, reminders for preparation of materials, off-campus events, and links to other pages for details. Each FLC on the MeetingMaker calendar appears in a different color for easy identification.

According to reports from FLC facilitators, the greatest hindrances to FLC participation are time and timing. Finding a time when all members of

NEW DIRECTIONS FOR TEACHING AND LEARNING, no. 97, Spring 2004 © Wiley Periodicals, Inc.

Figure 7.1. Sample Calendar for All Miami FLCs

April 2003				◁▼ ▼	Today ▲ ▲ ▲|
Monday	Tuesday	Wednesday	Thursday	Friday	
	1 8:00 CELT Committee Meeting	2 4:00 CELT Seminar—Recognition 5:00 1st Wed Gathering	3 3:00 American Studies FLC Revising the Curriculum	4 🖰 Lilly East @ Towson, MD	
7 12:00 Writing FLC 4:00 Teaching Scholars FLC	8 12:00 Arts in the Curriculum FLC 4:00 Technology FLC 7:00 p.m. Department Chairs FLC	9 1:00 US Cultures FLC 6:00 CELT & Lilly Reunion Potluck	10 🖰 AAC&U 5:30 PFF FLC	11 🖰 AAC&U 1:00 US Cultures FLC 4:00 Small Group FLC	
14 6:00 Humanities & Digital Technology FLC	15 8:00 a.m. Writing FLC Closing Retreat 4:00 Technology FLC	16 11:30 Assessment FLC 4:00 CELT Seminar 7:00 Teaching Scholars FLC	17 8:00 a.m. CELT Committee Meeting	18	

a group can meet is a continual struggle, even after the group decides on a time for themselves. Disciplinary conferences, manuscript due dates, and family obligations can throw off the best-laid plans. One method is to send community members a schedule form on which to mark off the times when they are not available during the week and to indicate any dates during the year when they know in advance they will not be available. This needs to be done each term, because faculty teaching and committee schedules change. Another option is to state in the call for applications for each FLC the days, dates, and times of meetings so that participants know in advance what times they need to reserve for FLC meetings and activities.

In addition to scheduling FLC meetings, a manager of multiple FLCs is responsible for travel arrangements, reports, communication, publicity, and maintaining the program's Web site. Publicity, including both printed materials and Web sites, needs to be designated for maximum appeal across disciplines.

Budgeting, purchasing, and bookkeeping for multiple FLCs require both a structured reporting system and a computerized accounting system. If FLC members are given funds with which to purchase transportation, equipment, or supplies, it is tempting to transfer the funds to accounts in the participants' departments. However, some participants do not use all their funds or may select unacceptable items to purchase. Thus, it is recommended that all purchases go through the central FLC manager. Both Miami University and Claremont Graduate University use FileMaker Pro for financial tracking for their FLC participants and facilitators.

Scheduling and Hosting. Scheduling rooms, audiovisual equipment, catering, and setup for the many meetings requires good relationships with all of the academic units and departments involved. The type and nutritional value of food—and when it is served—are key elements of FLCs because food sets the tone and energy of the meeting. Meals need to be light enough to keep the participants alert and must be provided at the most productive time. In addition, hosting seminars and events involves preparation of invitations, materials, sign-in sheets, name tags, decorations, photography, follow-up evaluations, and other details. The central manager also schedules, purchases tickets for, and prepares reimbursements for faculty travel to FLC-related conferences and retreats.

Database Management. The ability to handle the many details involved in managing multiple FLCs often depends on the accessibility and flexibility of the database used. FileMaker Pro is used at Miami University to integrate data on individual faculty members (see Figure 7.2 for an example) with attendance, budget, and other essential information. Claremont Graduate University's FLC office uses Microsoft Access to maintain records on its FLC participants and activities.

Figure 7.2. Sample FLC Database Page

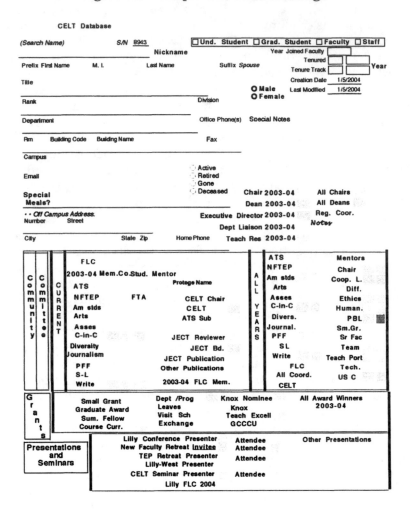

Interpersonal Connections with FLC Facilitators and Participants

With multiple FLCs comes the opportunity to meet and work with innovative and enthusiastic faculty and staff. If one is managing ten FLCs, the number of these colleagues can be over a hundred. A combination of firmness and graciousness are needed to handle budget, scheduling, and due date extension requests (as well as FLC members who do not RSVP). The management role also may include being a patient listener, as some FLC colleagues may encounter obstacles in their personal or academic lives. A positive, "can do" attitude by support staff is an important asset in establishing FLC networks across campus.

MELODY AYN BARTON is administrative associate in the Center for the Enhancement of Learning and Teaching at Miami University, where she also is earning her master's degree in college student personnel. She has managed the logistics, catering, personnel, budgets, and publicity for over fifty FLCs (six to eleven per year).

LAURIE RICHLIN is director of the Claremont Graduate University Preparing Future Faculty and faculty learning communities programs and director of the Lilly Conference on College and University Teaching–West. She has managed eleven FLCs and facilitated six.

Evaluation and assessment are critical to the success of FLCs, and authentic assessment has the potential to contribute greatly to the quality of FLC experiences in terms of both process and outcomes.

Assessing Faculty Learning Communities

Harry Hubball, Anthony Clarke, Andrea L. Beach

This chapter focuses on evaluation and assessment issues and practices within the context of faculty learning communities (FLCs). We define evaluation and assessment and their roles in the sustainability of FLC programs, then focus on authentic assessment and examine the ways in which it can shape the quality of FLC experiences. In particular, we explore metacognition as a central construct underlying authentic assessment—a construct that we argue is critical to but often absent from many descriptions and analyses of assessment practices for FLCs. We follow this with an examination of guiding principles for authentic assessment. Finally, we provide a conceptual framework and practical applications for assessing FLCs.

The issues we explore in this chapter complement the arguments presented for FLCs and their ongoing development in the other chapters of this sourcebook. The increasing attention educational developers are giving to the value of FLCs in higher education, as well as our extensive work with a particular FLC at the University of British Columbia, calls for greater scrutiny of evaluation and assessment practices in FLC contexts.

Evaluation and Assessment of FLCs: An Overview

Evaluation is generally defined as "the systematic investigation of the worth or merit of an object" (Joint Committee on Standards for Educational Evaluation, 1994, p. A3). It focuses on the effectiveness of programs and is guided by predetermined goals and priorities. In the context of FLCs, evaluation focuses on the effectiveness of an FLC program in meeting the goals set by the institution and program coordinators. Assessment is the systematic

NEW DIRECTIONS FOR TEACHING AND LEARNING, no. 97, Spring 2004 © Wiley Periodicals, Inc.

gathering of information about component parts of the thing being evaluated, and therefore the assessment of learning—of faculty participants, the FLC as a collective, the FLC facilitators, and, ultimately, the students—forms the core of effective evaluation of FLC programs. Ultimately, FLCs focus on improving student learning through improved faculty teaching. As such, assessment of student learning is a key (though challenging) element in the assessment of FLCs. Individual faculty learning outcomes and FLC outcomes form another level of assessment. Both inform the larger evaluation of programs with multiple FLCs. Audiences for this assessment and evaluation include potential participants and internal institutional stakeholders such as department chairs, deans, and academic administrators, all of whom might potentially provide financial support for FLC efforts. Evaluation and assessment are therefore key to the long-term success and sustainability of FLCs. They provide information on processes to FLC facilitators and program directors for the purpose of program improvement, and information on outcomes to institutional stakeholders for the purpose of decision making in regard to continued support.

A growing body of literature in higher education points to the importance of authentic assessment (Angelo and Cross, 1993; Paris and Ayres, 1994; Shavelson and Huang, 2003; Wiggins, 1990). Authentic assessment is designed to address learning that is meaningful to the learner and the skills and abilities needed to perform actual or real-world tasks. In contrast, traditional assessment measures learning in ways important to or convenient for faculty and institutions but may be quite disconnected from the real-world application of learning. Among the demonstrations of performance used in authentic assessment of student learning are such activities as simulations, group projects, experiments, demonstrations, interviews, essays and other writing samples, oral presentations, observations, and the construction of portfolios. In the context of FLCs, authentic assessment would address the learning important to faculty (for example, new teaching approaches that encourage active learning and authentic assessment in their own classroom) and the FLC as a whole (for example, collaborative learning about the nature of learning and teaching) in addition to the student learning that is the ultimate intended outcome. We argue that assessment of FLCs should be guided by the well-defined principles of authentic assessment (Angelo and Cross, 1993; Paris and Ayres, 1994; Shavelson and Huang, 2003; Wiggins, 1990) and also build on the unique characteristics of an FLC environment. Authentic assessment is perhaps the single most powerful mechanism that can shape the quality of FLC experiences.

Metacognition: A Defining Feature of Authentic Assessment Practices Within FLCs

We begin our discussion of authentic assessment by addressing a key concept that guides our thinking and use of such practices—namely, that of metacognition ("learning how to learn") as it applies to the individual and

**Figure 8.1. An FLC Environment Based on a Traditional View
of Teaching and Learning**

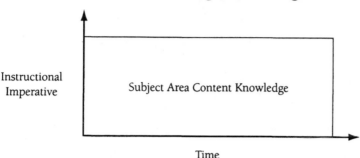

Instructional
Imperative   Subject Area Content Knowledge

Time

collective dimensions of FLCs. Essentially, metacognition embraces a broader and richer conceptualization of authentic assessment by adding a level of self-reflection on learning that other conceptions do not and is grounded in the FLC context of self-regulated learning practices (Glassick, Huber and Maeroff, 1997; Johnson, 2002). Individual faculty members, as well as the FLC as a whole, need to understand how they learn best within particular contexts in order to successfully engage in authentic assessment. Therefore, learning must involve both metacognitive and subject-specific content knowledge as they relate to the abilities, skills, and experiences of the participants.

To illustrate metacognition in relation to authentic assessment, we contrast two hypothetical FLC learning environments. The first represents a traditional view of teaching and learning. The second embraces metacognition as an essential element of the teaching and learning environment. While our descriptions represent extreme cases, we have drawn these extremes deliberately to differentiate the instructional imperatives that define the two FLC environments. In the first learning environment (Figure 8.1), instructional emphasis is placed on content coverage—no more, no less—in the time allotted for faculty learning. Faculty members are expected to reproduce specific content knowledge on demand—for example, at the end of a professional development workshop or at the completion of a certificate program. We suspect that this rendering of an FLC will resonate with some readers who know colleagues who subscribe to this approach in their own classrooms or administrators who exhibit this approach during faculty retreats or curricular reviews.

Now consider an FLC in which, in the eyes of the FLC facilitator, metacognition plays an important role in faculty learning. In this FLC (Figure 8.2), the facilitator believes that faculty learning of content is intimately related to the metacognitive abilities of the faculty members—that is, the way in which faculty understand how they learn, both individually and collectively (Devine, 1993; Schoenfeld, 1987). The instructional

Figure 8.2. Metacognitive FLC Environment

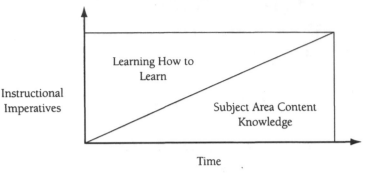

imperatives in this environment, then, are twofold: metacognitive and content-specific (knowledge, abilities, and skills).

Valuing metacognition means that professional development time in FLCs must be shared between presenting content knowledge and allowing faculty the opportunity to develop metacognitive skills (Cox, 1999). This claim is based on the proposition that the more metacognitive skills that faculty have, the less time facilitators need to spend on subject-specific content knowledge. Faculty with metacognitive skills have a greater capacity, individually and collectively, to engage with content knowledge and therefore require less in-house time to address the specific content knowledge associated with, for example, a particular professional development initiative. Figure 8.2 also illustrates that for facilitators to fully reap the rewards of a metacognitive learning environment, they need to front-load FLC programs with opportunities for participants to develop metacognitive skills. Therefore, the metacognitive component takes precedence early in their engagement with an FLC.

Opportunities to develop metacognitive skills range from faculty explorations of their own (and others') learning styles to individual and collaborative activities that embrace the full spectrum of learning strategies that faculty bring to bear on their own learning (Gunstone and Mitchell, 1998; White and Mitchell, 1994). Once faculty have been exposed to learning environments that emphasize the importance of metacognition and become comfortable with those skills, the metacognitive dimension can be reduced somewhat (see Figure 8.3), but metacognitive development should remain an important and critical component of FLC activity. Authentic assessment of and within FLCs depends on the degree to which metacognition is a significant feature of the instructional imperatives of the FLC—be it in a study group or a certificate program—and the degree to which faculty exhibit metacognitive abilities as a result of the FLC's activities.

Figure 8.3. A Metacognitive FLC Environment in Which Faculty Already Have an Appreciation of the Metacognitive Dimension

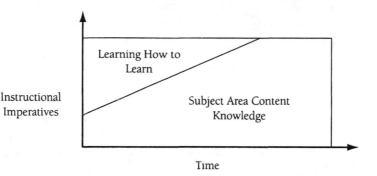

Guiding Principles for Authentic Assessment of FLCs

We propose three principles that build on the metacognitive foundation outlined above and bring to life authentic assessment within FLC contexts. In developing these principles, we have drawn on the work of a number of authors (for example, Angelo and Cross, 1993; Baker, O'Neill, and Linn, 1993; Cox, 1999, 2001, 2003; Newmann and Associates, 1996; Wiggins, 1989, 1998).

• *Authentic assessment requires faculty members to be actively engaged in the process.* For example, faculty should be expected to provide input with regard to setting objectives for FLCs, identifying appropriate assessment strategies and criteria to evaluate process and outcome issues, and participating in assessment experiences that require faculty members to think critically and engage in self-directed learning (individually and collaboratively).

• *Authentic assessment should take place in a variety of carefully planned ways before, during, on completion of, and following the FLC experience.* This principle can be applied on many levels—by faculty members to assess the impact of their learning projects on student learning in their classes; by faculty members to assess their own learning; by FLC facilitators to assess their own and faculty learning; and by the FLC collectively to assess their processes and outcomes—using a wide range of informal (question-and-answer, reflection, or review of classroom discussion and group work) and formal (written or oral examination and critique of final product, questionnaire surveys, focus groups, or Web and document examination and reflection) methods of assessment over the course of the FLC.

• *Authentic assessment of FLCs is both an individual and social contextual process.* Requiring faculty participants to engage in a program that balances independent (self-reflection, individual feedback, goal setting and self-monitoring) and collaborative (group goal setting and analyses, peer review) assessment strategies is more likely to engage diverse learning styles within a faculty cohort and enhance a sense of community among learners while providing a balance of preferred and challenging experiences for each faculty member. This mix will enable individuals to develop a broad set of knowledge, abilities, and skills (Kolb, 1984; Kolb and Boyatis, 2001; Gardner, 1993).

These principles are consistent with contemporary assessment approaches for FLCs and translate directly into working techniques. For example, at Miami University and other institutions that have adopted the FLC model, faculty are involved in deciding what gets studied, what projects participants will pursue, and how participants will assess the implementation of their projects with the students in their focus courses. In addition, FLC members themselves reflect and offer feedback to one another on their learning throughout the course of the year. They complete surveys that were developed through years of experience and participant input at Miami University and that ask them to reflect on their own learning. FLC facilitators complete a similar questionnaire assessing their roles and learning. As a result of the Ohio Learning Network (OLN) Learning Communities Initiative (Chapter Six), members of each FLC collaboratively compile a year-end report of their activities and learning and create a case study report on their experiences based on their reflections on the processes and outcomes of their FLC (see Appendix A at the end of this chapter). These principles also guide our work at the University of British Columbia to ensure that the metacognitive dimension is honored within the context of the Faculty Certificate Program on Teaching and Learning in Higher Education. The degree to which these principles are negotiated and employed within the context of FLCs will often determine the extent to which authentic assessment practices are implemented.

A Framework for Assessing FLCs

The following framework embraces the three principles for authentic assessment of FLCs and was developed by adapting concepts and strategies from Green and Kreuter's (1999) model for program planning and evaluation. This flexible and iterative framework takes context into account and integrates responsive organizational strategies for assessing FLCs. Practical strategies for each component of the framework are drawn from a combination of literature sources and practical experiences with FLCs.

FLC context strategies take into account the big picture and critical motivational factors when building teams and crafting responsive assessment strategies to enhance the effectiveness of FLCs. Conducting a comprehensive needs assessment with faculty participants, educational developers, and administrators should reveal critical information about the institutional culture around teaching and learning issues, as well as the required resources that would contribute to the implementation of a successful FLC. For example, consultation dialogue, and collaboration with

FLC members can help to ensure that assessment not only is meaningful and relevant to the needs and circumstances of FLC members but also is manageable to administer and, above all, enhances the process and outcomes of the FLC (Baker, 1999; Barab and Duffy, 2000; Caffarella and Zinn, 1999; Cox, 1999; Green and Kreuter, 1999; Hansman, 2001; Nolinske, 1999).

Planning strategies refer to developing clearly defined learning objectives for the FLC and scheduling systematic short-term and long-term assessments at critical times (for example, before, during, and on completion of the FLC process and at follow-up intervals). Learning objectives, in large part, should inform and guide FLCs (Baird, 1996; Lockhart and Borland, 2001).

Data collection strategies refer to the range of methods (for example, self-reflection, focus group interviews, meeting notes, projects, portfolios, faculty presentations, surveys) employed to gather information pertaining to FLC process and outcome issues. Data collection should include informal and formal opportunities for self, peer, and facilitator feedback over the full course of the FLC (Angelo and Cross, 1993; Cox, 2003; Harper, 1996). For example, within the Miami University FLCs and the five institutions that have adopted the FLC model under the FIPSE grant, participants' self-report data is gathered with scaled and open-ended questions regarding the perceived impacts of FLCs on student learning and their own professional development. Collaborative methods of data collection in this FLC context include the use of the OLN case method instrument mentioned earlier (Appendix A). This method is particularly useful for building community within the FLC at incremental stages in the process because it asks members to reflect together on their process and outcomes.

Interpretation strategies refer to the development of criteria in order to make appropriate judgments about the impact on FLC objectives of various FLC processes, including members' individual contributions to the FLC, and about how well long-term outcomes have been achieved. Drawing on clearly defined criteria and a variety of data sources will result in more valid and reliable judgments about FLC processes and outcomes (Brown, Bull, and Pendlebury, 1997; Fenwick and Parsons, 2000; Green and Kreuter, 1999; Richlin and Manning, 1995).

Authentic Assessment and FLCs: The UBC Faculty Certificate Program on Teaching and Learning in Higher Education

The framework of FLC context, planning, data collection, and interpretation strategies was applied to the eight-month Faculty Certificate Program on Teaching and Learning in Higher Education (FCP) at the University of British Columbia (UBC). For example, the FCP began in 1998 and was designed to meet the needs and circumstances of a cross-disciplinary cohort of faculty members at various ranks who are involved in teaching or curriculum development at UBC. The aim of the FCP is to help provide faculty with knowledge, abilities, skills, and experiences to enhance the scholarship of teaching and learning at UBC.

The certificate program focuses on a set of clearly defined learning outcomes. On completion of the certificate program, faculty are expected to be able to think critically about curriculum and pedagogical issues in higher education; articulate their own values and beliefs about teaching and learning; recognize the value of inclusion, student equity, and diversity; design responsive courses and assess student learning using a variety of methods; facilitate active learning, critical thinking, and problem solving; develop a critically reflective teaching practice; and use a variety of communication, teamwork, and leadership skills. A metacognitive disposition is explored, encouraged, and supported throughout the FLC activities.

Faculty members participate in the FCP as part of a cohort and engage in both collaborative and independent learning experiences. Using the results of a prior learning assessment (PLA) interview and a needs assessment survey, each faculty member follows an independent learning plan that combines theory, practice, and critical reflection pertaining to a wide range of integrated learning experiences, including action research, peer review of teaching practices, discussion forums, peer workshop presentations, and constructing a teaching dossier. Authentic assessment is an integral part of learning throughout the FCP. To address diverse learning styles within a cross-disciplinary cohort, successful completion of program learning objectives are demonstrated through an array of assessment methods (Table 8.1), crafted at strategic times throughout the program of study. Again, the development of metacognitive skills pervades these practices. For example, during the initial PLA, participants are encouraged to think about and make explicit their preferred learning styles.

Authentic assessment strategies are deployed at crucial points during the FCP: prior learning assessment, formative, summative, and at follow-up stages. Prior to the program, as part of a focused needs assessment survey, all FCP participants meet individually with FLC facilitators to discuss pedagogical needs and interests, prior learning experiences, and program goals and to develop independent learning plans based on their learning styles. During the program, formative assessment occurs via ongoing feedback related to workshop presentations, teaching dossiers, program portfolios, and program evaluations. These assessment strategies require substantive reflection pertaining to a wide range of curricular, teaching, and learning issues. In addition to self-assessment, feedback is provided by peers within the cohort and by instructors to individual faculty participants at key stages of the program, keeping in mind the many ways in which people learn. Appendix B provides guidelines for assessing teaching dossiers and portfolios. At the end of the FCP, a summative assessment driven by specific criteria occurs in the form of an interview with a peer who is external to the

Table 8.1. Individual and Collaborative Methods of Assessment

Assessment Method	Learning Experience
Instructor feedback	Prior learning assessment interview to identify needs, learning styles, interests, and teaching development goals; workshop presentations; formative and summative feedback and progress check of ILP and cohort contributions
Self-assessment reflections	Each workshop and learning experience; teaching dossier and program portfolio development; program attendance and contribution to cohort; formative and summative ILP and program evaluations
Peer feedback	Workshop presentations; action research assignments; program attendance and contribution to cohort; teaching dossier and course syllabus
External peer review	Postprogram learning interview and review of ILP, teaching dossier, and program portfolio materials by previous graduates

program. This assessment strategy focuses on the quality of teaching dossiers or portfolios and progress throughout the FCP. Finally, the assessment cycle is completed after the program when past participants complete a survey questionnaire to formally evaluate the quality of the FCP, as well as to reflect on the application of their own learning. The impacts of FLC strategies for developing the scholarship of teaching and learning in the FCP are examined by Hubball (manuscript completed Oct. 2003), who describes the research designs and results in detail.

The authentic assessment strategies within the FCP produced the following suggestions: organize an FLC around issues relevant to cross-disciplinary faculty members; ensure that the pedagogical environment closely simulates the university teaching and learning context; engage faculty as stakeholders in the FLC process and outcomes; enhance the quality and quantity of the FLC contributions by individual faculty members and thereby improve the quality of FLC experiences; and reinforce the successful modeling of FLC assessment strategies and assignments within student classrooms. Authentic assessment has the potential to meet the diverse needs and circumstances of a cross-disciplinary faculty cohort by engaging participants in a learning community and by drawing on a wide range of abilities and collaborative and independent learning experiences.

Conclusion

Authentic assessment practices for FLCs require FLC facilitators and program directors to have a desire for lifelong learning, a diverse range of skills and abilities that facilitate their own and others' learning, an ability to create an inclusive learning environment, the willingness to develop assessment activities that allow for differentiated responses from individuals and groups, as well as to monitor and evaluate the effectiveness of the FLC—all attributes that FLCs themselves aim to develop in faculty. By basing authentic assessment practices in metacognition, FLC facilitators and program directors model the kind of reflection in which they would like faculty participants to engage. Faculty in turn embed those metacognitive approaches and authentic assessment into their courses and model for students the kind of thinking that faculty wish them to develop. Authentic assessment, therefore, when carefully designed and facilitated, can provide an effective strategy that enhances FLCs and their impact on the learning of their students.

Authentic assessment also provides the rich information focused on faculty and student outcomes that evaluators of FLC programs need to justify their continuation to chairs, deans, and other academic administrators who are increasingly focused on cost-benefit ratios and shrinking budgets. The long-range success of FLCs depends on evaluation, and authentic assessment provides a framework that both respects and enhances the spirit within which FLCs have developed and facilitates the kinds of data collection that speak to the concerns of institutional decision makers for concrete outcomes.

Appendix A: FLC Case Study Report for Ohio Learning Network Learning Communities Initiative

Ohio Learning Network Learning Communities Initiative
Adapted for FIPSE Project

Learning From Experience: Developing Portraits of Practice
CASE RECORD, Part One

A. Institution's Name:
    FLC Name:
B. FLC Overview: Tell the world what you're doing. *75 words or less!*
C. Case Recorder(s): Identify the person(s) preparing the case record on behalf of the FLC. *Who are you?*
D. FLC Members, Units, Roles:
    List your community members, their units or disciplines, and roles in the learning community. *Who are core members and associates (key people involved in the community project other than core members) of your learning community? What experiences do each bring to the community and project?*
    Other comments about FLC members and supporters:
E. Background and Context:
    Briefly describe your learning community project, opportunity, or purpose and the context within which you undertake it. *What do you hope to achieve? How will this contribute to learning at your institution? What desired ending(s) would you like for the story of your learning community and its project? What types of institutional support do you have or would you like?*

F. Description of your early work, planning and preparations:
Describe the preliminary work of the learning community as you prepare for your community project and for attending your learning institute. *What were the key components in your planning and preparation for your learning community? (roles? methods? time lines? coordinating schedules?) What were key issues and concerns, and how did you sort them out? What were the key successes and what impact have they had? Are there any vignettes that illustrate these?*

G. Description and learning about your community building and project development:
Describe early phases of building your community and developing the project. *What key challenges, problems, solutions, struggles, and failures do you have and how do you handle them? What did they—or will they—lead to? What successes have you enjoyed to date? Are there any vignettes about potential consequences or impacts that you can share? How are you using the learning communities information provided?*

Learning From Experience: Developing Portraits of Practice
CASE RECORD, Part Two

H. Description and reflections on implementation:
Describe the test or trial and interactive phases of your project, including impact on learning. Use critical incidents and vignettes to illustrate the action of your community's project. *What are key challenges, problems, solutions, struggles, and failures, and how do you handle them? What have been your key successes? How have you leveraged these to your advantage?*

I. Key Resources:
Who and what are the people, organizations, materials, Web sites, and other resources you utilized? What types of support did you receive from your departments, colleges, administration? Of all resources, which were essential?

J. Discussion:
This is your opportunity to capture the conversations among learning community members as all of you reflect critically on the community and your project. As you reflect back on the preliminary stages of your community and its focus area and how it has evolved and developed over time, what are critical incidents, key questions, and junctures that made a difference in how the community and your project evolved? What worked, and why do you think it worked? What didn't work, and why do you think it didn't work? What are your overall conclusions?

What are the next steps in the cycle of reflective practice? It is possible that the next steps cannot be predicted and may take you in another fruitful direction?

How might your Case Record be used as a resource for other individuals and communities?

What questions/issues might you pose to the reader of your Case Record to help in their efforts?

Appendix B: Teaching Dossier Guidelines and Evaluation Criteria

Components
- Teaching Dossier (4–10 pages: Abilities, Accomplishments, Aspirations)
- Teaching Dossier Appendices (4–10 pages: supporting documentation)

Teaching Dossier: Reflective Analysis
  Introduction
  Table of contents; relevant education and experience for university teaching; context of university teaching; brief overview of teaching dossier

Approach to Teaching and Learning
    Philosophy of teaching and how students learn (beliefs, ethics, values, intentions);
teaching and learning strategies employed; TREK 2000 integration
Major Teaching Contributions
    Teaching responsibilities, supervisory roles, professional development leadership,
committee service, administrative activities, publications, Web-based materials, and
innovations related to curriculum and pedagogy
Assessment of Teaching: Critical Reflections
    Critique methods used to assess teaching; results of teaching and teaching evalua-
tions (formative and summative student feedback); accomplishments (awards); teaching challenges and strategies; summary statement and goals (short-term and long-term)
for further development

Appendices: Supporting Documentation (4–10 pages)

Teaching Dossier Evaluation Criteria
Self, Peer, Instructor Assessment: Pass Criteria
Quality of Presentation
    Portfolio is clearly organized, with table of contents, materials complete in each
section, and appropriate style, format, and structure
Consistency
    Connections drawn and a clear match between philosophy, practice, major teach-
ing contributions, and assessment of teaching
Quality of Evidence
    Originality, creativity, innovation; worthy claims supported by credible, reliable,
authentic, and varied data sources
Quality of Analysis
    Level of reflection and planning for further development demonstrates rigor, accu-
racy, self-expression, and perspective

References

Angelo, T. A., and Cross, K. P. *Classroom Assessment Techniques: A Handbook for College Teachers.* (2nd ed.) San Francisco: Jossey-Bass, 1993.
Baird, L. L. "Documenting Student Outcomes in Graduate and Professional Programs." In J. G. Haworth (ed.), *Assessing Graduate and Professional Education: Current Realities, Future Prospects.* New Directions for Institutional Research, no. 92. San Francisco: Jossey-Bass, 1996.
Baker, E. L., O'Neill, H. F., Jr., and Linn, R. L. "Policy and Validity Prospects for Performance-Based Assessments." *American Psychologist,* 1993, 48, 1210–1218.
Baker, P. "Creating Learning Communities: The Unfinished Agenda." In B. A. Pescosolido and R. Aminzade (eds.), *The Social Worlds of Higher Education.* Thousand Oaks, Calif.: Pine Forge Press, 1999.
Barab, S. A., and Duffy, T. "From Practice Fields to Communities of Practice." In D. Jonassen and S. M. Land (ed.), *Theoretical Foundations of Learning Environments.* Mahwah, N.J.: Erlbaum, 2000.
Brown, G., Bull, J., and Pendlebury, M. *Assessing Student Learning in Higher Education.* London: Routledge, 1997.
Caffarella, R., and Zinn, L. "Professional Development for Faculty: A Conceptual Framework of Barriers and Supports." *Innovative Higher Education,* 1999, 23(4), 241–254.
Cox, M. D. "Peer Consultation and Faculty Learning Communities." In C. Knapper and S. Piccinin (eds.), *Using Consultation to Improve Teaching.* New Directions for Teaching and Learning, no. 79. San Francisco: Jossey-Bass, 1999.

Cox, M. D. "Faculty Learning Communities: Change Agents for Transforming Institutions into Learning Organizations." *To Improve the Academy,* 2001, *19,* 69–93.

Cox, M. D. "Proven Faculty Development Tools That Foster the Scholarship of Teaching in Faculty Learning Communities." *To Improve the Academy,* 2003, *21,* 109–142.

Devine, J. "The Role of Metacognition in Second Language Reading and Writing." In J. G. Carson and I. Leki (eds.), *Reading in the Composition Classroom: Second Language Perspectives.* Boston: Heinle and Heinle, 1993.

Fenwick, T., and Parsons, J. "Developing Criteria for Evaluation: Choosing a Frame of Reference." In T. Fenwick and J. Parsons (eds.), *The Art of Evaluation: A Handbook for Educators and Trainers.* Toronto: Thompson Educational Press, 2000.

Gardner, H. *Multiple Intelligences: The Theory in Practice.* New York: Basic Books, 1993.

Glassick, C. E., Huber, M. T., and Maeroff, G. I. *Scholarship Assessed: Evaluation of the Professoriate.* San Francisco: Jossey-Bass, 1997.

Green, L. W., and Kreuter, M. *Health Promotion Planning: An Educational and Ecological Approach.* (3rd ed.) Palo Alto, Calif.: Mayfield, 1999.

Gunstone, R., and Mitchell, I. "Metacognition and Conceptual Change." In J. Mintzes, J. Wandersee, and J. Novak (eds.), *Teaching Science for Understanding.* San Diego, Calif.: Academic Press, 1998.

Hansman, C. A. "Context-Based Adult Learning." In S. B. Merriam, (ed.), *The New Update on Adult Learning Theory.* San Francisco: Jossey-Bass, 2001.

Harper, V. "Establishing a Community of Conversation: Creating a Context for Self-Reflection Among Teacher Scholars." *To Improve the Academy,* 1996, *19,* 251–266.

Hubball, H. "A Faculty Learning Community Within a Certificate Program: Enhancing the Scholarship of Teaching and Learning." Unpublished manuscript, Oct. 31, 2003.

Johnson, E. B. *Contextual Teaching and Learning: What It Is and Why It's Here to Stay.* Thousand Oaks, Calif.: Corwin Press, 2002.

Joint Committee on Standards for Educational Evaluation. *The Program Evaluation Standards.* Thousand Oaks, CA: Sage, 1994.

Kolb, D. A. *Experiential Learning: Experience as the Source of Learning and Development.* Englewood Cliffs, N.J.: Prentice Hall, 1984.

Kolb, D. A., and Boyatis, R. E. "Experiential Learning Theory: Previous Research and New Directions." In R. J. Sternberg and L. Zhang (eds.), *Perspectives on Thinking, Learning, and Cognitive Styles.* Mahwah, N.J.: Erlbaum, 2001.

Lockhart, M., and Borland, K. W. "Critical Thinking Goals, Outcomes, and Pedagogy in Senior Capstone Courses." *Journal of Faculty Development,* 2001, *18*(1), 19–25.

Newmann, F. M., and Associates. *Authentic Achievement: Restructuring Schools for Intellectual Quality.* San Francisco: Jossey-Bass, 1996.

Nolinske, T. "Creating an Inclusive Learning Environment." *Teaching Excellence,* 1999, *11,* 4.

Paris, S., and Ayres, L. R. *Becoming Reflective Students and Teachers with Portfolios and Authentic Assessment.* Washington, D.C.: American Psychological Association, 1994.

Richlin, L., and Manning, B. *Improving a College/University Teaching Evaluation System.* San Bernardino, Calif.: Alliance, 1995.

Schoenfeld, A. H. "What's All the Fuss About Metacognition?" In A. H. Schoenfeld (ed.), *Cognitive Science and Mathematics Education.* New York: Erlbaum, 1987.

Shavelson, R. J., and Huang, L. "Responding Responsibly to the Frenzy to Assess Learning in Higher Education." *Change,* Jan.–Feb. 2003, pp. 11–18.

White, R. T., and Mitchell, I. J. "Metacognition and the Quality of Learning." *Studies in Science Education,* 1994, *23,* 21–37.

Wiggins, G. "A True Test: Toward More Authentic and Equitable Assessment." *Phi Delta Kappan,* 1989, *70,* 9.

Wiggins, G. "The Case for Authentic Assessment." *Practical Assessment, Research and Evaluation,* 1990, *2*(2).

Wiggins, G. *Educative Assessment: Designing Assessments to Inform and Improve Student Performance.* San Francisco: Jossey-Bass, 1998.

HARRY HUBBALL is assistant professor in the Department of Curriculum Studies and co-chair of the Faculty Certificate Program on Teaching and Learning in Higher Education at the University of British Columbia.

ANTHONY CLARKE is associate professor in the Department of Curriculum Studies at the University of British Columbia.

ANDREA L. BEACH is assistant professor in the Department of Teaching, Learning, and Leadership at Western Michigan University.

Technology can be used to effectively support FLCs. This chapter explores how technology and a community of inquiry model can be used to facilitate individual reflection and critical discourse about teaching practice.

Technology in Support of Faculty Learning Communities

Norman Vaughan

A recent study by the American Association for Higher Education (Rice, Sorcinelli, and Austin, 2000) suggests that early-career faculty "want to pursue their work in communities where collaboration is respected and encouraged, where friendships develop between colleagues within and across departments, and where there is time and opportunity for interaction and talk about ideas, one's work, and the institution" (p. 13). The major challenge of sustaining such communities is always one of time. Increased teaching and research commitments leave new and experienced faculty with limited time for face-to-face professional development opportunities. The question then arises, can technology be used to create more flexible and accessible learning communities for faculty?

The follow-up survey of faculty learning communities (FLCs) across North America, described in Chapter Two, demonstrates that numerous higher education institutions are currently wrestling with this question of how technology can be used to extend the conversation within an FLC. The survey results indicate that 90 percent of the respondents (63 of 70) are using some form of computer-mediated communication, such as e-mail or online discussion groups, to support their FLCs. The specific tools include e-mail systems (98.4 percent), Web sites (49.2 percent), online discussion forum tools (42.9 percent), course management systems (27 percent), and virtual chat tools (7.9 percent).

NEW DIRECTIONS FOR TEACHING AND LEARNING, no. 97, Spring 2004 © Wiley Periodicals, Inc.

Blended Learning

Many students in higher education also are struggling with increased time pressures as they try to balance family and work commitments with their studies. A number of educational institutions in North America have responded to this concern by offering a series of courses in a blended for-mat (Twigg, 2003). The goal of these courses is to combine the best features of in-class teaching with the best features of online experiences to promote active learning and reduce seat time (Garnham and Kaleta, 2002). A pilot study was conducted at Mount Royal College in Calgary, Canada, to deter-mine whether this type of blended learning model could be effectively applied to FLCs through the use of educational technology.

Pilot Study Overview

The pilot study involved eleven faculty members who had applied to receive release time to learn how to integrate technology into their teaching prac-tice. The goal of this topic-based FLC was to provide faculty members with opportunities for sustained reflection and discourse about their teaching practice so that they each could create a Web site to support student learn-ing. The community met six times, on a biweekly basis, between January and March of 2003. Between these face-to-face sessions, participants engaged in a series of online activities (for example, computer-mediated dis-cussions and document sharing).

Community of Inquiry Model

Garrison, Anderson, and Archer's community of inquiry (CoI) model was used to guide the inquiry process within this FLC (Garrison, Anderson, and Archer, 2000). The CoI framework was originally developed to support a successful higher educational experience within a computer conferencing environment. The model is based on a collaborative constructivist perspec-tive of education, the integration of "personal reconstruction of experience and social collaboration" (Garrison and Archer, 2000, p. 11). This type of community of inquiry is described as follows:

> A critical community of learners, from an educational perspective, is com-posed of teachers and students transacting with the specific purposes of facil-itating, constructing, and validating understanding, and of developing capabilities that will lead to further learning. Such a community encourages cognitive independence and social interdependence simultaneously. [Garrison and Anderson, 2003, p. 23]

There are three core elements of this model: social, teaching, and cog-nitive presence. *Social presence* refers to the "ability of participants in a community of inquiry to project themselves socially and emotionally as 'real' people (i.e., their full personality), through the medium of communication being used" (Garrison, Anderson, and Archer, 2000, p. 14). *Teaching presence* includes the "design, facilitation, and direction of cognitive and social processes for the purpose of realizing personally meaningful and educationally worthwhile learning outcomes" (Anderson, Rourke, Garrison, and Archer, 2001, p. 1). *Cognitive presence* is described as "the extent to which learners are able to construct and confirm meaning through sustained reflection and discourse in a critical community of inquiry" (Garrison, Anderson, and Archer, 2001, p. 11).

When this model is applied to an FLC, the focus of the cognitive presence becomes an inquiry process into teaching practice. The ability of the community to support and sustain this inquiry forms the social presence. And the opportunities for blended (face-to-face and online) learning are encapsulated within the teaching presence. The Venn diagram in Figure 9.1 and categories in Table 9.1 illustrate how this community of inquiry model can be extended to an FLC.

Figure 9.1. Community of Inquiry Model Applied to an FLC

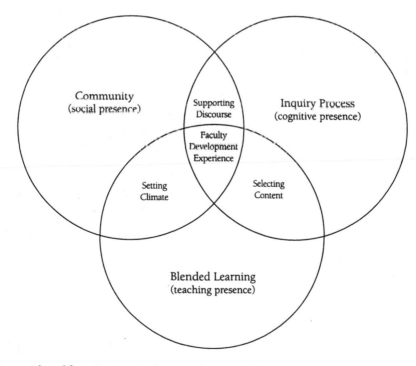

Source: Adapted from Garrison, Anderson, and Archer, 2000.

Table 9.1. Community of Inquiry within an FLC

Sphere	Description	Category/Phase	Indicators
Inquiry process (cognitive presence)	The extent to which faculty are able to construct and confirm meaning through sustained reflection, discourse, and application within a critical community of inquiry.	1. Triggering event 2. Exploration 3. Integration 4. Resolution/application	1. Inciting curiosity and defining key questions or issues for investigation 2. Exchanging and exploring perspectives and information resources with faculty colleagues 3. Connecting ideas through individual project construction 4. Applying new ideas directly within teaching practice
Community (social presence)	The ability of faculty in a community of inquiry to project themselves socially and emotionally as real people (that is, their full personality) through the medium of communication being used. Faculty learn best from each other.	1. Establishing trust and respect 2. Open communication 3. Group cohesion	1. Expressing emotions 2. Risk-free expression 3. Fostering collaboration
Blended learning (teaching presence)	The design, facilitation, and direction of the inquiry and community processes for the purpose of realizing personally meaningful and educationally worthwhile learning outcomes for faculty within an environment that carefully integrates face-to-face and online sessions and activities.	1. Organizing and designing the faculty development program 2. Facilitating discourse within the community 3. Providing direct instruction for faculty participants	1. Setting curriculum and methods 2. Stimulating and sustaining the sharing of personal meaning and insights 3. Modeling and focusing discussion, activities, and project construction

Source: Adapted from Garrison, Anderson, and Archer, 2000.

Pilot Study Results

Surveys, poststudy interviews, and a focus group were conducted to compare the face-to-face and online sessions within this FLC. The data indicated that the ongoing face-to-face sessions allowed personal relationships and a sense of community to develop. This, in turn, fostered the sharing of ideas and experiences among the participants. Garrison, Anderson, and Archer (2000) add, "socially and emotionally, face-to-face oral communication is a rich medium" (p. 6). However, several faculty members stated that they found communication in the face-to-face sessions to be less systematic, more exploratory, and less attentive to the perspective of others than computer-mediated communication.

The online component of the blended design created an opportunity to extend and sustain the dialogue and sense of community. In addition, the faculty participants commented on the reflective nature of asynchronous (not-at-the-same-time) online communication. The computer-mediated discussion forums allowed participants to reflect individually about their teaching practice through the process of composing messages to their peers. They were then exposed to other perspectives, different from their own, through reading discussion forum postings from other members of the community.

There are those who suggest that this emphasis on the written word encourages a deeper level of thinking (Weigel, 2002). As well, the realization that the thoughts expressed in these discussion postings "will be exposed semi-permanently to others . . . seems to result in a deeper level of discourse" (Smith, Ferguson, and Caris, 2001, p. 5). Garrison, Anderson, and Archer (2000) indicate that the literature suggests "that written communication is very closely connected with careful and critical thinking" and "that it is the reflective and explicit nature of the written word that encourages discipline and rigor in our thinking and communicating" (p. 6).

Despite these positive outcomes, the biggest challenge encountered within this pilot study was getting faculty to participate in the online component of the blended design. The study participants were very eager to attend the face-to-face sessions but less willing to engage in the online learning activities. Post-study interviews revealed that some of the reasons for this reticence in the online environment were a lack of familiarity with online communication, the lower value placed on this form of communication, electronic communication overload, and the option to delay communication until the face-to-face sessions.

Pilot Study Recommendations

The faculty participants unanimously agreed that the online activities greatly benefited their learning in the FLC, and they generated a series of potential strategies for overcoming what they referred to as "online apathy." These strategies included an initial orientation to online communication and a requirement that all community members be involved in the design and facilitation of the online activities. Participants suggested that at the beginning of the FLC program, the facilitator should provide a hands-on orientation to the specific computer-based communication tools to be used (for example, a course management system like WebCT or Blackboard) and start an online discussion thread in which participants would introduce themselves. Participants also recommended that time be provided within each face-to-face session for faculty to begin their online activities.

Other recommendations included the involvement of all community members in the selection of topics and the development of questions for the online activities, to ensure relevance and interest for the entire group. The community also should develop its own set of guidelines and criteria for online participation, and each participant should be encouraged to moderate a discussion forum about a topic or issue of interest in order to gain experience as a moderator. In addition, the facilitator should continually emphasize to the FLC members that through participation in the online activities, they will gain further insight into what it is like to be a learner in an online environment.

Finally, the participants stated that educational technology should be used to facilitate online activities before and after each face-to-face session in order to sustain continual cycles of inquiry within an FLC. North American survey respondents (see Chapter Two) reported that a number of higher education institutions are currently using Web-based course management systems to support a variety of online activities for their FLCs. These course management systems provide the capability for online threaded discussion forums, real-time chats, whiteboards, assessments, surveys, calendars, collaborative work groups, and content repositories. Table 9.2 outlines how Web-based activities can be used to foster inquiry cycles within an FLC.

Conclusion

The initial findings from the North American survey and the pilot study reveal that technology can be used to effectively support FLCs by creating new opportunities for individual reflection and critical discourse about teaching practice. Without proper planning, technology can become a disconnected add-on, creating a sense of frustration and loss of time rather than learning opportunities for participants within an FLC. To successfully use technology to achieve FLC goals, thoughtful and systematic planning (for example, for the use of technology to support inquiry cycles) is required to ensure that the face-to-face and online sessions are successfully integrated.

Table 9.2. Using Technology to Support Inquiry Cycles Within a Faculty Learning Community

Sequence	Event	Purpose	Use of Technology
1. Before session	• Individual prereading assignment or activity on a specified topic or issue, followed by • Web-based self-assessment quiz or survey	Learner • Create a triggering event that simulates recall of prior learning experience • Advance organizer such as a quiz stimulates connections Facilitator • Determine participants' prior knowledge or experience with the topic or issue	• Pre-reading or activity can be Web-based (for example, a digital learning object such as an animation or video clip) • Construction and utilization of a Web-based self-assessment quiz or survey
2. During session	Roundtable discussion (face to face) • Dialogue with facilitator and fellow learners about the specified issue or topic Computer lab • Sharing of existing project examples and resources • Minitutorial followed by hands-on time for project building related to topic • Anonymous exit survey: What did you learn? What are you still not clear about?	Roundtable discussion • Defining the triggering events (key questions) • Beginning to explore the questions Computer lab • Further exploration and a start toward tentative integration through the ability to connect theory to practice	Roundtable discussion • Display the class results for the self-assessment quiz or survey Computer lab • Display project examples and resources • Software resources • Anonymous exit survey

Table 9.2. (Continued) Using Technology to Support Inquiry Cycles Within a Faculty Learning Community

Sequence	Event	Purpose	Use of Technology
3. After session	Week One Online discussion • Post results of anonymous feedback survey • Member of the group moderates the discussion (choice of activity) • Summary of the discussion created for next session Week Two • Individual prereading assignment or activity on the next topic or issue, followed by • Web-based self-assessment quiz or survey	Further exploration and tentative integration	• Online discussion forum • Online bulletin board for posting the discussion summary • Prereading or activity can be Web-based (for example, a learning object) • Construction and utilization of a Web-based self-assessment quiz or survey
4. Next session	Roundtable discussion (face to face) • Final group thoughts on first topic or issue • Review of online discussion summary • Begin the dialogue for next topic or issue	Integration and tentative resolution	• Cycle begins again

References

Anderson, T., Rourke, L., Garrison, D. R., and Archer, W. "Assessing Teaching Presence in a Computer Conferencing Environment." *Journal of Asynchronous Learning Networks,* 2001, 5(2).

Garnham, C., and Kaleta, R. 'Introduction to Hybrid Courses." *Teaching with Technology Today,* 2002, 8(6).

Garrison, D. R., and Anderson, T. E. *Learning in the 21st Century: A Framework for Research and Practice.* London: RoutledgeFalmer, 2003.

Garrison, D. R., Anderson, T., and Archer, W. "Critical Thinking in a Text-Based Environment: Computer Conferencing in Higher Education." *Internet and Higher Education,* 2000, 11(2), 1–14.

Garrison, D. R., Anderson, T., and Archer, W. "Critical Thinking, Cognitive Presence, and Computer Conferencing in Distance Education." *American Journal of Distance Education,* 2001, 15(1), 7–23.

Garrison, D. R., and Archer, W. *A Transactional Perspective on Teaching and Learning: A Framework for Adult and Higher Education.* New York: Elsevier Science, 2000.

Rice, R. E., Sorcinelli, M. D., and Austin, A. E. *Heeding New Voices: Academic Careers for a New Generation.* New Pathways: Faculty Careers and Employment for the 21st Century Series, Working Paper Inquiry no. 7. Washington, D.C.: American Association for Higher Education, 2000.

Smith, G. G., Ferguson, D., and Caris, M. "Teaching College Courses Online Versus Face-to-Face." *T.H.E. Journal,* 2001, 28(9), 15–18.

Twigg, C. "Improving Quality and Reducing Cost: Designs for Effective Learning." *Change,* July–Aug. 2003, pp. 23–29.

Weigel, V. B. *Deep Learning for a Digital Age: Technology's Untapped Potential to Enrich Higher Education.* San Francisco: Jossey-Bass, 2002.

NORMAN VAUGHAN is coordinator of educational technology integration in the academic development center at Mount Royal College.

*Both in structure and focus, FLCs create a necessary
construct for a cultural transformation of teaching and
learning that invites all to achieve their intellectual
and social potential.*

Supporting Diversity with Faculty Learning Communities: Teaching and Learning Across Boundaries

Martha C. Petrone

An Allegory: Rehgih Noitacude

Rehgih Noitacude is a long-established culture that is insulated from the outside world. It prides itself on its sophisticated language, elaborate rituals and traditions, unique artifacts and ceremonial dress, and elite values and beliefs. At the same time, recognizing the need to adapt to the changing world, Rehgih Noitacude has begun to open its borders to the Srenruojos.

There is great enthusiasm among the Srenruojos who enter this culture, for they feel it offers many opportunities to enrich their lives; yet when they arrive, they quickly experience culture shock. The ways in which things are done are foreign to them. Far from feeling accepted, the Srenruojos feel compelling pressure to conform to a disturbing range of ambiguous norms and unstated rules. The Srenruojos want to fit in, but not at the cost of their own cultural identity. Because Rehgih Noitacude doesn't feel safe or welcoming to them, they find solace in this strange and lonely place by banding together. With varying success, Rehgih Noitacude continues to attempt to do what it can to help them adjust to their new environment, but many feel the Srenruojos may just be too different.

The Reality

It seems that nearly every article on diversity in higher education today begins with startling statistics about the changing demographics in the United States and the urgent need for higher education to respond to them. A comparison of the U.S. Censuses for 1990 and 2000 documents 57.5 percent, 21.5 percent, and 74.3 percent increases in the Hispanic or Latino, African American, and Asian American populations, respectively (U.S. Census Bureau, 2001). Furthermore, projections indicate that within the next twenty years, 47 percent of the population growth in the United States will be among Latino Americans, 22 percent will be among African Americans, and 18 percent will be among other minority group members. Once the bastion of the elite, higher education is now an accessible and necessary option for high school and nontraditional students—many from diverse backgrounds—who display a formidable array of cognitive modes, communication styles, and cultural values.

Over the last forty years, colleges and universities have responded to these demographic shifts in a number of ways, including targeted recruitment, special mentorship programs, efforts to create more inclusive campus climates, and curricular and pedagogical transformation. In many of these initiatives to get more underrepresented students and faculty into the academic pipeline, the focus is on social justice and equity. While this orientation helps to advance the democratic goals of higher education, active engagement with diversity both in and outside of the classroom also promotes deeper levels of critical thought and social development (Hurtado, 1999). Gloria Ladson-Billings states, "[Critical] pedagogy operates in the realm of the relational and societal. No longer are we referring merely to knowledge transactions that occur in the classroom but the larger societal meanings that are imparted between and among teachers, students, and their social worlds" (Ladson-Billings, 2002).

Deeply rooted in American values and an individualistic cultural tradition, higher education emphasizes personal accomplishments over those of the group. In contrast, collectivistic cultures value group welfare over individual rights and needs. Based on cultural tendencies, women, Latino, Asian, Native American, and, to a lesser extent, African American students and faculty are socialized in collectivistic cultures wherein collaboration rather than competition serves as the energizing force and underlying identity value. To those with collectivistic cultural identities, higher education can be an unwelcoming and disorienting place. The learning community model encourages necessary institutional cultural transformation by inviting students and faculty to cross social, disciplinary, pedagogical, and curricular boundaries and by recognizing diversity as a core component of a liberal education (Decker-Lardner, 2003).

Faculty learning communities (FLCs)—whether based in a cohort of new, midcareer, female, or minority faculty or focused on a topic such as a particular pedagogical approach or curricular development—serve as a transdisciplinary space for meaningful, ongoing discussion of innovative ways to effectively address the teaching and learning needs of increasingly diverse student populations. As their long-term goals suggest (see Chapter One), FLCs also provide a collaborative framework for participants' own development and create a necessary collectivistic shift in the academic culture. As FLCs build universitywide community, incorporate ways that difference can enhance teaching and learning, increase faculty collaboration, and encourage reflection about the coherence of learning across disciplines, they contribute to the overarching objective of enabling the university to become a learning organization (Cox, 2001).

Seminars on multiculturalism and pedagogical and curricular approaches abound in higher education. They provide useful information and potential points of entry for understanding and change. However, successful pedagogical and curriculum innovations require faculty to traverse the dialectic between the traditional and the transformed (Vavrus, 2002). In FLCs, through the ongoing interaction with colleagues from other disciplinary and cultural perspectives, faculty members operate in a multicontextual construct (Ibarra, 2001). By negotiating this individualism-collectivism identity continuum with their colleagues, they gain heightened awareness of their own and others' social behavior. This intrapersonal and interpersonal knowledge facilitates improved practice in integrating diversity into the existing curriculum, pedagogical approaches, and classroom settings.

FLC Impact on Diversity

As Richlin and Essington describe in Chapter Two, a survey was sent to respondents at 132 institutions that were identified as having FLCs, asking questions about the impact of FLC participation on incorporating diversity into teaching. Responses reflected a range of perspectives. Several respondents mentioned that they learned most about "understanding of diverse ways of knowing," "learning styles," and "various ways individuals not only learn but excel." Others wrote specifically about the impact of class and age on their students' learning. Several identified specific differences based on their FLC topic; for example, a participant in an FLC on writing-intensive courses stated, "I thought it was interesting to see how the various disciplines think of writing. I remember when the chemists in our group realized that writing was actually a means of learning. It was like a light bulb went on and they thought differently thereafter about their writing assignments."

The most frequently reported teaching adjustments included "assignment planning" and "ways to assess learning." One respondent reported, "I have decreased the amount of group work with classes that typically have younger students. Mature students seem to be more focused and have better outcomes with group work. I have increased the number of assessments in several courses in order to provide more frequent feedback and therefore more positive outcomes. I have also increased the amount of group work that takes place during class in some courses in order to promote critical thinking and problem solving in a more structured setting."

The most important effect reported by respondents was that they now are better able to consider many aspects of their students in planning and implementing their courses. One wrote, "I am more aware of the different needs of my community college students (who are all so diverse)." Another wrote:

> Throughout my participation in this experience, I continually asked myself, "Will this work with OUR student population?" I thought about groups of students that I have taught in the past and currently and how my methods have had to shift with different groups. These shifts will always continue throughout my teaching career because the student populations change. I guess I just got more of a sense of the need to continually reassess who it is I am teaching and be flexible about my approaches.

Each FLC, evolving from institutional needs for change, serves as a laboratory for faculty engagement and introspection about diverse ways of knowing, learning, and teaching. Some responses to the survey implied that the extent of engagement with diversity issues was in part dependent on the diversity of the participants or the students they teach. At the same time, it is quite possible that a teacher could engage issues of difference and multiculturalism with a culturally very uniform class, while conversely, another teacher could go to great lengths to ignore such issues in a very diverse class. This raises the following question: "What approaches can institutions take to engage faculty more directly in efforts to enhance their intercultural understanding of diverse others as well as themselves, thereby leading to significant changes in the teaching and learning setting?" Through a synergy of structure and focus, FLCs on diversity topics can be the answer.

The Diversity FLC and the Cultures FLC at Miami University

Despite Miami University's reputation for academic excellence, efforts to recruit and retain minority and international students and minority and female faculty had historically been unsuccessful (Center for the Study of Higher and Postsecondary Education, University of Michigan, 1996). Given the degree of homogeneity among the faculty and student body, the university recognized that in order to transform the institutional culture, faculty would have to embark on a journey of personal exploration of their own attitudes toward the centrality of diversity in the education process. In 1997, in response to this objective and the growing body of literature about the impact of diversity on teaching and learning, the university initiated the

Faculty Learning Community Using Difference to Enhance Teaching and Learning (Diversity FLC). Specific objectives of this FLC included (1) to increase awareness and understanding of who we are (and the impact we have on the teaching and learning process), (2) to recognize differences and similarities among our students and between our students and ourselves, (3) to explore pedagogies and behaviors that create an inclusive classroom culture, and (4) to investigate curriculum development involved in moving toward more diverse and inclusive course content (http://www.units. muohio.edu/celt/community-difference.shtml).

The Faculty Learning Community on U.S. Cultures Course Development (Cultures FLC) also was created to meet an institutional need, but it had a different genesis and direction. This FLC, jointly sponsored by the Liberal Education Council and the Committee for the Enhancement of Teaching and Learning, offered faculty an opportunity to participate in a collective investigation and dialogue with other colleagues who were developing course proposals for a new U.S. Cultures Requirement. As part of the Miami Plan—a liberal education curriculum for all students—the objectives for these courses included (1) course content reflecting multiple perspectives, (2) pedagogies that create inclusive classroom climates, (3) activities and strategies for fulfilling the four tenets of the Miami Plan (thinking critically, understanding contexts, engaging with other learners, and reflecting and acting) and (4) techniques for assessing the success of these courses in achieving student learning outcomes connected with multicultural teaching and learning (http://www.units.muohio.edu/celt/ community-uscultures.shtml).

The following quotation from an FLC participant in the 1999–2000 Diversity FLC expresses the sentiments of many in both diversity communities:

> I joined this FLC to find ways to incorporate diverse perspectives in my courses. However, my participation in this community provided me with much more than that. It has had a profound effect not only on how I see the teaching and learning setting but also on my worldview and probably more importantly, how I see myself both as a teacher and a person.

Throughout the six-year life of these FLCs, the program director and facilitators also learned a great deal about the unique dynamics and interventions necessary for topic-based FLCs on diversity. Using the collective experience from these Miami University FLCs and two FLCs on Multicultural Course Transformation (Multicultural FLCs) at Indiana University–Purdue University Indianapolis, the next section highlights specific strategies, significant outcomes, and important considerations in implementing and facilitating FLCs on diversity. The following list enumerates these lessons, along with related key questions and possible approaches for addressing them.

The Top Ten Things We Have Learned About FLCs on Diversity (So Far)

1. *An FLC on diversity must operate on both emotional and intellectual levels.* Because of our positions as experts in our fields, we, as faculty, often retreat to the intellectual level and want quick answers and ready solutions. How do we, as faculty who are expected and accustomed to focusing on the cognitive domain of learning, tap the affective and psychomotor domains in our own teaching and learning? How can we facilitate the integration of all three domains into the teaching and learning setting?

Planned experiences that move faculty members outside of their comfort zone help to create learning through action and affect. For example, in addition to attending a conference together to provide a knowledge base, integrating related social and educational activities into the trip agenda provides participants with a community context for their learning.

As part of a conference trip to Philadelphia, participants in the 1998–99 Miami University Diversity FLC toured and did research at the Balch Institute for Ethnic Studies, met with leaders and attended a party at the William Way Gay Lesbian Transgender Community Center, and learned about conflict resolution and fair housing advocacy programs available at the Human Relations Commission. The next year, while attending the American Council of Education national conference, "Educating All of One Nation," held in Albuquerque, New Mexico, the Diversity FLC members celebrated the Day of the Dead at El Centro de la Raza (the Spanish-speaking student center at the University of New Mexico), met with the president and the executive director of the Hispanic Chamber of Commerce, and made a site visit to the historic mission of Santoria de Chimajo. The 2000–01 Diversity FLC members, along with twenty-eight students, went to Miami, Oklahoma, to attend the annual Miami Indian Stomp Dance and the opening ceremony for the new Miami Indian Childcare Center there. Much like a service-learning pedagogy, as opposed to cultural tourism, these experiences connect theory to practice through linkage of the cognitive with the psychomotor and affective domains of learning.

2. *As faculty, we need to unpack our "briefcases of professorial privilege,"* just as McIntosh (1989) asks us to unpack our knapsack of white privilege. There appears to be a pervasive attitude that diversity education and multicultural awareness is something our students and less enlightened colleagues require. Faculty who apply to an FLC on diversity may consider themselves part of the "choir." But faculty development must emphasize that ethnocentrism and "educentrism" exist on a continuum and are filters through which we all view the world. To effectively integrate other voices into our courses and classroom, we must be willing to learn more about our own preferences, biases, and privilege as faculty members regardless of how much we already think we know or do. How do we examine our own predispositions based on upbringing and culture and their impact on the

teaching and learning setting? In what ways do we expect students to know how to think, write, act, or respond to their discipline and to our teaching methods based on our personal educational preparation and learning preferences?

On an individual level, student associates are invaluable resources for faculty in FLCs focusing on diversity. It is important to recognize that some faculty may not be receptive to this idea. Therefore, student associate involvement must depend on the comfort level of the individual faculty member and can range from providing feedback on specific aspects of class content, materials, or pedagogical strategies to coteaching a course.

On a group level, ongoing contact and dialogues with student organizations for underrepresented groups can have a meaningful impact on FLC participants. In the early years of the Miami University program, FLC members decided to tour the Center for Black Culture and Learning (CBLC). Afterward, a couple of the participants pointed out that they never got to actually meet with the students who used the facility to find out what they thought of their educational experience and the teaching and learning climate at Miami. Together with student leaders, the facilitators arranged for this conversation to occur. Eight faculty members and approximately fifteen African American students engaged in a dynamic and enlightening conversation about their intellectual and social experiences at our institution. It was an eye-opener. FLC members maintained contact with the CBLC and some of the students throughout the academic year and beyond. In subsequent years, Diversity FLC members maintained a yearlong connection with the Gay Lesbian Bisexual and Transexual Alliance, the Asian American Student Union, and the Native American Student Association.

Through significant interpersonal and group connections with students, faculty negotiate the individualism-collectivism dialectic and gain valuable insights into the impact of their own personal perspectives and preferences with regard to teaching and learning while relinquishing some of their professorial privilege. One Diversity FLC participant stated, "I have identified [some of] my own biases and some inclusive strategies that I can apply. This self-assessment has been invaluable."

The author has developed two inventories to facilitate this reflection—one to help faculty members assess their own inclusiveness"(Appendix A) and one with which students can assess classroom climate (Appendix B).

3. *FLCs on diversity need to promote both awareness and implementation of what is learned.* Although an increased awareness of what will work more effectively in a multicultural environment is important, it must be balanced with tangible evidence of the ways in which faculty implement this knowledge in their courses and classrooms and with what impact. What are the desired learning outcomes and how will we assess them most effectively?

Diversity is a highly abstract concept. Within an FLC of eight persons, there are likely to be just as many definitions of diversity. Although faculty may agree that it is about otherness, in order to implement a project with meaningful educational outcomes, they must move beyond this vague conceptualization to specifically frame their research questions, identify goals and objectives, and then translate them into tangible and measurable outcomes (Anderson, 2002).

Through exposure to the scholarship of teaching and learning about identity development theory for diverse types of students, faculty members can identify benchmarks in how others have targeted specific student populations, researched their perspectives, and implemented and assessed innovative pedagogies. One Diversity FLC participant indicated, "Background information was good, but I am not certain if I know how to apply it" and expressed a desire for "sample curriculum that would serve as examples for what is expected in integrating concepts."

These varied resources provide faculty with methods to assess the validity of their assumptions, to gain a multidimensional picture of diverse ways of knowing, to supplement the cognitive with the experiential, and to monitor constantly for bias within and around them (Sue, 1999) while providing pilot models for curricular change.

The call for applications for the Cultures FLC included three expected outcomes designed to create intrainstitutional resources. Participants were expected to (1) develop one or more course proposals for the U.S. Cultures requirement, (2) develop a course portfolio while teaching the course (and update the portfolio during subsequent offerings), and (3) serve as mentors to other faculty who are interested in developing courses to meet the U.S. Cultures requirement.

Members of the Cultures FLC developed or modified courses such as "Disability Studies," "Development, Learning, and Diversity: Multicultural Perspectives and Concerns," "Images of America," "American Politics and Diversity," "Psychology Across Culture," and "Strength Through Cultural Diversity." Furthermore, their course portfolios and personal experiences in developing and teaching the courses are available to any faculty interested in developing a U.S. Cultures course. The Cultures FLC members also expanded their roles as mentors to include dissemination of their work through presentations at the 2002 National Conference on Race and Ethnicity and the 2003 Lilly Conference on Teaching and Learning (Heuberger and others, 2003).

4. *There are "diversities of scale."* Some differences are perceived as greater than others, and people are more uncomfortable discussing them. While faculty may be comfortable discussing racism or sexism, they often avoid heterosexism and neglect ableism. Which aspects of others' identity dimensions are invisible to us? Which do we individually find most difficult to understand? Which identity dimensions make us uncomfortable and why?

Less visible underrepresented groups on college campuses often remain silent. A student with a learning disability may be embarrassed about not being like other students; a gay, lesbian, or questioning student may not be likely to call attention to an offensive remark; or a Jewish student may not feel free to express concern about an assignment due on a holy day.

Many colleges and universities have campus advocacy programs for students, often offered through the office or division of student affairs. At Miami University, a campuswide training program called Community Advocacy Alliance provides training and certification for campus "safe zones." FLC members attended this training. Not only did it help to enlighten them about the silent minorities on campus, but it encouraged them to develop constructive ways to handle conflicts that might arise in their classrooms. If such training is unavailable, an institution's diversity or inclusion statement is a good starting point for a discussion.

Auditing syllabi, classroom materials, and examples is another way to invite more voices into the classroom dialogue. By examining and discussing ways that underrepresented students are either excluded or invisible in classroom content, the primary identity dimensions of all students can be recognized, acknowledged, and incorporated.

5. *Faculty can make their courses more inclusive in a range of ways,* which I denote thus: $I = P \times C^3$: Inclusion equals Pedagogy times Content, Construction, and Climate. How can faculty from all disciplines transform their courses and pedagogy to include all voices?

All faculty can use teaching methods to facilitate the learning of all students, integrate a variety of examples and information about diverse groups into the course content and curriculum, address how knowledge is created and influenced by the eight identity dimensions of age, race, ethnicity, sex, gender, religion, ability, and class, or construct classroom climates in which all students regardless of their differences are encouraged to achieve their maximum potential both academically and socially (Banks, 1999). One Diversity FLC participant stated, "I have become much more aware of the need to understand and specifically state the expected student outcomes in the syllabus as well as in class. I have also become aware of the need to focus on the diversity and multicultural issues that may exist in the classroom as well as their relevance to class content."

Up to now, the Top Ten List has dealt with the broad issues that may be an FLC on diversity. The rest of these lessons focus on the role of the facilitator in encouraging the work of the group.

6. *Efforts to collectively establish FLC ground rules and model conflict resolution skills are best done up front.* Doing so helps to create an environment in which participants feel safe to share and encourages a genuine exchange of perspectives. How do we begin to talk about talking about difficult subjects? What guidelines can we establish to provide room for all voices?

At the opening retreat of each of the Diversity FLCs, the cofacilitators led the members in an exercise designed to establish group objectives and ground rules for engaging together to fulfill them. "Talking About Talking About" is a simple but effective way to establish ground rules while raising an issue that the FLC is likely to have to grapple with as a group (Petrone,

2002). For example, the facilitator might share the following quotation with the FLC members.

> The dominant communication framework in the United States values explicit verbal messages which calmly and objectively express personal opinion. For those from collectivistic cultures, however, ideas are expressed, often with feeling, in a circular pattern where the main point is often left unstated and the meaning of the message is derived from the context of what is said. [Hall, 1976]

In what ways have we seen this dynamic play out in our classes or committee meetings? What can we do to address it in our own future interactions with each other?

Another method of setting group goals and ground rules is to pose a series of climate-setting questions for participants to answer individually and then share with the entire group. For example, questions might include "What needs to happen in the course of this FLC to make your commitment of time and energy worthwhile?" "What are you personally willing to do to make this happen?" and "What can the rest of us do to help you achieve your objectives?" (Reddy, 1996).

In addition to establishing parameters for the interactions within the FLC, the process of establishing group ground rules serves as a model for engaging difficult topics within the classroom.

7. *Often the dynamics in the greater university or culture play out in the FLC.* How do we encourage participants to ask themselves, "Do I listen completely for understanding before expressing myself?" "When I share my thoughts, do I express them as my perspective, leaving open the possibility there may be others besides mine?"

For example, a remark may be construed as sexist by another participant, or an Asian participant may feel that a European American dominates the discussion and does not wait long enough to allow others to respond and express themselves. In such situations, the FLC facilitator or other participants can draw on the established ground rules and encourage participants to recognize these situations without attacking, judging, or blaming. A dialogue based on listening first and then expressing thoughts, feelings, and experiences will help participants gain clearer insight into their own behavior and the effect it may have on others.

8. *Diversity topics require more direct intervention from the facilitator.* Although faculty members engage with their disciplines at deep levels of thought, they may not be engaged at a deep level with their own worldview. Are participants avoiding the deeper issues and instead asking for "just what they need to know for the 'test'" in engaging with others from different traditions, backgrounds, and perspectives from their own?

The six stages of the Developmental Model of Intercultural Sensitivity help to explain this phenomenon. Developed by Milton Bennett (1993), the underlying assumption of this analytical framework is that as an individual's experience with culture becomes more sophisticated, the potential for a more expansive worldview increases. The first three stages of the model depict the ethnocentric perspectives of denial, defense, and minimization, with the final three encompassing the ethnorelative stages of acceptance, adaptation, and integration (Bennett, 1993). The first three stages are often seen as ways of avoiding cultural difference, whereas the last three stages are ways of seeking cultural difference. Just as students need encouragement to engage with various disciplines at more complex levels, FLC participants often require the skills of an FLC facilitator to help them move further along the continuum of intercultural sensitivity, regardless of where their perspective falls on it.

Double-loop learning is based on the examination of underlying assumptions and values and exploration of other possible perspectives (Pedersen, 1996). Unlike single-loop learning, this approach is based on designing and facilitating learning situations or environments in which participants (1) can examine core values orientations that may lead to biases that might undermine student success, (2) accept mutual responsibility and accountability for a safe setting that protects both the self and others, and (3) work together to reduce personal and organizational defensiveness against change (Argyris, 1985; Fulmer, 1998; Paul, 2003).

9. *Civility expressed as silence can be interpreted as neutrality, creating a defensive reaction and a diminished sense of inclusion in the FLC.* What is not being discussed that should be? Is energy being drawn off-line? At times, diversity issues can be uncomfortable for the FLC participants. When that happens, there is a tendency toward avoidance and apparent neutrality that draws energy from the group and its work. Like a teacher in a classroom, a facilitator models the role of group process consultant by monitoring and acknowledging how members of the group relate to one another and by guiding the content, planning, and outcomes for the FLC. As a result of participating in the Diversity FLC, one member noted:

> I think I became braver about approaching sensitive subjects that students might be reluctant to discuss. I found when I confronted an issue, students then became more willing to talk about that issue. . . . I think that all students in that class are more accepting of multiculturalism than they once were. I [also] think that . . . I relate better to students from minority cultures; it is terribly important for a teacher to be visibly fair with all students and to model behaviors so the students know the expectations for civility in all circumstances.

10. *Avoid the lure of "diversity clutter"* (Edgar Beckham, consultant, quoted in Climate Committee, Miami University, 2003). As the body of knowledge and the number of campuswide diversity and multicultural initiatives increase, the FLC may find it difficult to reach consensus on specific

individual and collective foci. There is also a tendency to undertake too many activities and projects, leading to potentially incomplete and disintegrated outcomes. By reemphasizing the overriding goal of increasing students' intellectual and social development, the facilitator assists the participants in setting realistic and attainable goals for incorporating difference in teaching and learning.

The Allegory Revisited

By forming small communities of learners, members of the Rehgih Noitacude are working together to achieve a better understanding of themselves, their culture, and the renovations necessary to make Rehgih Noitacude a place where all Srenruojos feel welcomed, valued, and able to achieve the goals they set for their own lives. These community members realize that it will take some time to transform the culture but feel enriched by their experience as a community and the ways it has changed them as well as Rehgih Noitacude. I conclude this chapter with their words:

> We developed a strong sense of community as the members found that others shared and supported their ideas and plans. The community became an ongoing reassurance of the value of the work and the need for extra effort such work requires. The sharing of information and experiences developed a sense of increasing expertise and confidence on the part of the members. . . . Some of the struggles have focused on frustrations members encountered in getting others to engage in the transformations being developed. We have turned these frustrations into a resolution to create a reflective piece on how doing this work challenges and changes the people who do it.

Appendix A: Self-Assessment Inventory on Inclusiveness

SELF-ASSESSMENT INVENTORY ON INCLUSIVENESS

Part I. Using the continuum below, please identify your response to each of the following statements. Write the number that corresponds to your response in the blank preceding each question. In order for this inventory to be useful, it is important that you answer as you believe you truly are.

5 Almost always   4 More often than not   3 Sometimes
   2 Not usually   1 Seldom, if ever

___ 1. I am comfortable interacting with others who are not my age, race, gender, religion, economic status, sexual orientation, or at my educational level.
___ 2. I am mindful of my speech and behavior in an effort to avoid offending others.
___ 3. I recognize the unique influence that my upbringing and education have had on my values and beliefs.
___ 4. I ask questions until I am sure I understand what others are saying.
___ 5. I am attentive to others' reactions when I am speaking to them.
___ 6. When I need assistance, I am comfortable asking for it.

___ 7. I listen with interest to those whose ideas differ from mine.

___ 8. If I were at an event with people who differed from me, I would make every effort to talk with them.

___ 9. I make a conscious effort to recognize when I stereotype.

___10. I like hearing all sides of an issue before making a decision.

___11. I adapt well to change and new situations.

___12. I enjoy people watching and try to understand the human dynamics in interactions.

___13. I can readily identify the personal biases I have toward others.

___14. People are generally good, and I accept them as they are.

___15. I try not to assume anything.

Part II. Now consider your responses in the context of your classroom interactions. Is your behavior different in that setting than in your day-to-day encounters?

Appendix B: Student Assessment of Classroom Climate

STUDENT ASSESSMENT OF CLASSROOM CLIMATE

Directions: Circle the number that corresponds to your response to each of the following statements.

5 Almost always   4 More often than not   3 Sometimes   2 Not usually
  1 Seldom, if ever

1. I felt welcome in this class.   5   4   3   2   1
2. The course policies and procedures were clear to me.
   5   4   3   2   1
3. The teaching methods helped me to meet my learning needs.
   5   4   3   2   1
4. I was treated as an individual in this class.
   5   4   3   2   1
5. There were assignments that matched my learning style.
   5   4   3   2   1
6. The examples were relevant to my life experience.
   5   4   3   2   1
7. The instructor encouraged the expression of different perspectives and worldviews.
   5   4   3   2   1
8. I felt able to express my own views openly.
   5   4   3   2   1
9. The language used in this class was appropriate and inclusive.
   5   4   3   2   1
10. Insensitive behavior or language was addressed appropriately.
   5   4   3   2   1
11. Conflict was handled in a constructive and respectful manner.
   5   4   3   2   1
12. I felt I could be myself in this class.
   5   4   3   2   1
13. The classroom atmosphere contributed to my ability to learn more effectively.
   5   4   3   2   1
14. Group work encouraged me to work better with those who are different from me.
   5   4   3   2   1
15. I felt a part of a community of learners in this class.
   5   4   3   2   1

References

Anderson, J. "A Discussion of Diversity and Learning Communities Must Incorporate Assessment." Presentation at the American Association of Higher Education Assessment Conference, Boston, June 2002.

Argyris, C. *Strategy, Change and Defensive Routines.* Boston: Pitman, 1985.

Banks, J. "Multicultural Education: Development, Dimensions, and Challenges." In J. Q. Adams and J. R. Welsch (eds.), *Cultural Diversity: Curriculum, Classroom and Climate.* Macomb: Illinois Staff and Curriculum Developers Association, 1999.

Bennett, M. J. "Toward Ethnorelativism: A Developmental Model of Intercultural Sensitivity." In R. M. Paige (ed.), *Education for the Intercultural Experience.* (2nd ed.) Yarmouth, Maine: Intercultural Press, 1993.

Center for the Study of Higher and Postsecondary Education, University of Michigan. *Miami University Campus Climate Survey.* Oxford, Ohio: Miami University, 1996.

Climate Committee, Miami University. *Annual Report of the Climate Committee.* Oxford, Ohio: Miami University, May 2003.

Cox, M. *Designing, Implementing, and Leading Faculty Learning Communities: Enhancing the Teaching and Learning Culture on Your Campus.* Sourcebook from the 2nd annual Lilly Conference on College and University Teaching, Summer Institute, Ashland, Ore., June 2001.

Decker-Lardner, E. "Approaching Diversity Through Learning Communities." Washington Center Occasional Paper. Olympia: Washington Center for Improving the Quality of Undergraduate Education, The Evergreen State College, 2003.

Fulmer, R. "A Conversation with Chris Argyris: The Father of Organizational Learning." *Organizational Dynamics,* 1998, 27(2), 21–32.

Hall, E. *Beyond Culture.* New York: Doubleday, 1976.

Heuberger, B., Briscoe, M., Fitch, F., Greeson, L., Hieber, M., Hulgin, K., and Paternite, C. "It Takes a Faculty Learning Community: Creating and Implementing Innovative Diversity Courses Through Interdisciplinary Dialogue." Paper presented at the 23rd annual Lilly Conference on College Teaching, Oxford, Ohio, Nov. 2003.

Hurtado, S. "Reaffirming Educators' Judgment: Educational Value of Diversity." *Liberal Education,* 1999, 85(2).

Ibarra, R. *Beyond Affirmative Action: Reframing the Context of Higher Education.* Madison: University of Wisconsin Press, 2001.

Ladson-Billings, G. *Crossing over to Canaan: The Journey of New Teachers in Diverse Classrooms.* San Francisco: Jossey-Bass, 2002.

McIntosh, P. "White Privilege: Unpacking the Invisible Knapsack." *Peace and Freedom,* July/August 1989, pp. 10–12.

Paul, M. J. "Double-Loop Diversity: Applying Adult Learning Theory to the Cultivation of Diverse Educational Climates in Higher Education." *Innovative Higher Education,* Fall 2003, 281, 35–47.

Pedersen, A. "Double-Loop Thinking: Seeing Two Perspectives." In H. N. Seeyle (ed.), *Experiential Activities for Intercultural Learning.* Yarmouth, Maine: Intercultural Press, 1996.

Petrone, M. "Teaching and Learning as a Transactional Process." In G. S. Wheeler (ed.), *Teaching and Learning in College: A Resource for Educators.* (4th ed.) Elyria, Ohio: Info-Tec, 2002.

Reddy, B. *Group-Level Team Assessment.* San Francisco: Pfeiffer, 1996.

Sue, D. W. "Creating Conditions for a Constructive Dialogue on 'Race': Taking Individual and Institutional Responsibility." In J. Q. Adams and J. R. Welsch (eds.), *Cultural Diversity: Curriculum, Classroom and Climate.* Macomb: Illinois Staff and Curriculum Devleopers Association, 1999.

U.S. Census Bureau. "Population by Race and Hispanic or Latino Origin for the United States: 1999 and 2000." Census 2000 PHC-T-1. [http://www.census.gov/population/cen2000/phc-t1/tab04.pdf]. Apr. 2, 2001.

Vavrus, M. *Transforming the Multicultural Education of Teachers: Theory, Research, and Practice.* New York: Teachers College Press, 2002.

MARTHA C. PETRONE is coordinator of humanities and fine arts at Miami University–Middletown in Middletown, Ohio. At Miami University (Oxford, Ohio), she served as a consultant to the Faculty Learning Community on U.S. Cultures Course Development and as cofacilitator of the Faculty Learning Community Using Difference to Enhance Teaching and Learning.

*The scholarship of teaching and learning has been a
primary motivator and focus of faculty learning
communities. This chapter reports on the strategies,
processes, and activities that foster this scholarship in
FLCs.*

Developing Scholarly Teaching and the Scholarship of Teaching and Learning Through Faculty Learning Communities

Laurie Richlin, Milton D. Cox

Since the Carnegie Foundation's *Scholarship Reconsidered* (Boyer, 1990)
named "the scholarship of teaching" one of the four scholarships appropriate for the American faculty, administrators and faculty development professionals have struggled with how to encourage and prepare faculty to do
that type of scholarly work. Boyer states that teaching is "a dynamic
endeavor ... [that] must be carefully planned, continuously examined, and
relate directly to the subject taught" (Boyer, 1990, pp. 23–24). Kreber and
Cranton (forthcoming) contend that "the scholarship of teaching includes
both ongoing learning about teaching and the demonstration of teaching
knowledge." They state that faculty members who commit to the scholarship of teaching engage in three different kinds of reflection on both theory-
based and experience-based knowledge as it relates to questions of
instructional design, pedagogy, and the broader curriculum. Most important, they assert that "the scholarship of teaching includes ongoing learning about teaching and the demonstration of teaching knowledge."

The concept called the scholarship of teaching actually involves two different, but closely related, activities, *scholarly teaching* and a resulting *scholarship* (Richlin, 1993a, 1993b, 1998, 2001; Richlin and Cox, 1994), which
differ in both their intent and their products. Both scholarly teaching and the
scholarship of teaching are vital to the life of the academy. The purpose of

scholarly teaching is to affect the activity of teaching and the resulting learning, while the *scholarship of teaching* results in a formal, peer-reviewed communication in appropriate media or venues, which then becomes part of the knowledge base of teaching and learning in higher education.

Scholarship of Teaching and Learning Survey

Faculty learning communities (FLCs) provide an excellent structure to help faculty members develop scholarly teaching and create the scholarship of teaching and learning (SoTL), in part due to the deep learning that can take place in an FLC. As described in Chapter Two, a survey was sent to the 132 institutions with FLCs, asking whether their FLCs incorporate SoTL and, if so, which aspects they included. The list of aspects provided in the survey included course development, course redesign, teaching projects, on-campus and off-campus presentations, on-campus and off-campus publications, and teaching portfolios or course portfolios. An open-ended "other" category was provided so that additional SoTL activities could be listed, but no other categories of activities were reported. Only two institutions reported not having any scholarly teaching or scholarship of teaching activities. In one case, the FLCs have seminars and events but do not work on any projects. The other reported that they "do not incorporate SoTL on an intentional basis, although it happens occasionally." Results are shown in Table 11.1.

Table 11.1. Scholarly Teaching and Scholarship of Teaching and Learning Activities in Faculty Learning Communities

Any SoTL	84 out of 86 responses	97.7%
Scholarly Teaching Activity	*Number of Institutions Reporting Activity (out of 84)*	*Percentage of Institutions Reporting Activity*
Course		
Design	52	61.9
Redesign	61	72.6
Both	46	54.8
Teaching projects	51	60.7
Teaching portfolios or course portfolios	39	46.4
Scholarship of Teaching Activity		
Presentations		
On-campus	63	75.0
Off-campus	51	60.7
Publication		
On-campus	29	34.5
Disciplinary journal	33	39.3
Multidisciplinary journal	22	26.2
Other journal	6	7.1

Scholarly Teaching Activities in FLCs. With 72.6 percent, course redesign was the most frequently reported activity. Course design (61.9 percent) and teaching projects (60.7 percent) were next most frequent. Over half (54.8 percent) reported having both course design and course redesign activities. Teaching portfolios or course portfolios were reported by 46.4 percent of the institutions.

Scholarship of Teaching Activities in FLCs. Presentations, both on campus (75.0 percent) and off campus (60.7 percent), were the most popular scholarship of teaching activities reported. Publications were distributed across on-campus (34.5 percent), disciplinary (39.3 percent), and multidisciplinary (26.2 percent) journals. Only 7.1 percent reported publication in other types of journals. It was not reported to what extent these were refereed presentations or journals.

How FLCs Encourage Teaching Scholarship

Two programs provide examples of ways that institutions are encouraging faculty members to become scholarly teachers and contribute to the scholarship of teaching.

Miami University. The longest-running FLC programs are at Miami University, which began in 1978 with a three-year Lilly Endowment junior faculty grant (Cox, 1995). The Junior Faculty FLC Program won the 1994 Hesburgh Award and the FLC program won a 2003 Hesburgh Certificate of Excellence from TIAA-CREF, recognizing it as the best faculty development program enhancing undergraduate education in the United States. The Miami University program has included eighty-one FLCs of twenty-four types; twenty are topic-based, addressing a variety of topics each year, and four are cohort-based FLCs, which serve graduate students, junior faculty, senior faculty, and department chairs. FLC members participate in a two-semester series of special activities and pursue individual projects related to teaching. In addition, they present their projects on campus and at regional and national conferences, including the national Lilly Conference on College Teaching, which is held on the Miami University campus (Cox, 2001). In fact, former Miami FLC participants are overwhelmingly the presenters from Miami at the Lilly Conference; in 2003, 91 percent (thirty-nine of forty-three) of the Miami University presenters were former FLC members. Some FLC members have published their work in a variety of journals.

This high percentage of presenters engaging in SoTL from FLCs has happened in part because Miami University has developed a sequence of ten developmental steps that an FLC facilitator should incorporate into the FLC year to introduce and engage the participants in the scholarship of teaching and learning (Cox, 2003). Exhibit 11.1 describes the ten developmental steps and their SoTL results.

Claremont Graduate University. Because of the national awards and positive outcomes of the Miami University FLCs, Claremont Graduate

Exhibit 11.1. Ten Developmental Steps That Foster the Scholarship of Teaching and Learning in a Faculty Learning Community

Step 1: Application for FLC membership
- Applicants prepare a response to a question asking for preliminary ideas about an individual teaching and learning project.

Results: Addressing an observation—perhaps in an uninformed or indirect way—about a problem or opportunity in teaching-learning

Step 2: Early planning for the FLC
- FLC facilitator selects a community focus book that includes extensive references connected to the FLC topic. See Cox (2004) for a list of focus books used in Miami University FLCs.

Results: Connecting the FLC to the knowledge base of teaching and learning

Step 3: Opening/closing retreat before the start of the year
- Facilitator, new members, and graduating members discuss meaning and examples of scholarly teaching, the scholarship of teaching and learning (SoTL), and the ongoing cycle of scholarly teaching and SoTL.
- FLC facilitator distributes and discusses the focus book, a multidisciplinary book list for optional readings, and information about hot topics in SoTL as evidenced by Lilly Conference theme tracks (Cox, 2004).
- Facilitator, new members, and graduating members discuss the "Guidelines for the Design and Description of a Teaching and Learning Project" (Richlin, 2001, pp. 66–67).
- Graduating members present their projects to the new members and then consult in breakout groups.
- The new community plans the first-term activities and seminar and retreat topics.

Results: Making public through the authority of peers the ongoing cycle of scholarly teaching and SoTL; guiding SoTL research; connecting to a more extensive literature

Step 4: Participants prepare for and start the year
- Each FLC member selects one course that he or she is teaching in the upcoming term to be a focus course.
- Each participant searches for and reads articles to inform his or her teaching and learning in the focus course and project.
- Each individual designs and writes a description of his or her teaching and learning project.
- Each individual prepares an initial learning plan, placing his or her teaching and learning project in context with other FLC components and activities.

Results: Connecting SoTL to teaching practice; consulting the literature; choosing an intervention

Step 5: Seminars and retreat
- The facilitator prepares and distributes and the members read a booklet containing the initial learning plans, focus course syllabi, and the teaching and learning projects.
- An external consultant familiar with the difference between scholarly teaching and SoTL reads the teaching and learning projects and meets with each individual to sharpen research design.
- Each community member makes a short presentation to the FLC about his or her project, and the group discusses each project, making suggestions.

Results: Making public SoTL for peer review

Exhibit 11.1. (Continued) Ten Developmental Steps That Foster the Scholarship of Teaching and Learning in a Faculty Learning Community

Step 6: Working on projects during the year
- Participants investigate other pedagogical areas, looking for connections to their project.
- Individuals carry out their teaching and learning projects.
- Student associates or mentors consult.
- Participants assess student learning and other project outcomes.
- Facilitator, participants, and community consult about project outcomes.

Results: Progressing through the ongoing cycle: moving from scholarly teaching toward SoTL by "conducting systematic observation, documenting observations, analyzing results, obtaining peer evaluation, identifying key issues, synthesizing results" (Richlin, 2001, p. 59)

Step 7: Presentations during the second term
- Individuals, teams, and perhaps the entire community present their work at a campuswide teaching effectiveness retreat.
- Presenters incorporate feedback from peers at the campus sessions.
- Individuals, teams, and perhaps the entire community present at a national conference.
- Presenters incorporate feedback from the audience at the national conference.

Results: Presenting SoTL; peer evaluation

Step 8: The opening/closing retreat at the end of the year
- Graduating members present their projects to and consult with the new members.

Results: Teaching, mentoring, and making SoTL public

Step 9: Continuation of the project during the summer or the upcoming year
- Each individual may apply for and use a small grant or summer fellowship to continue his or her project on his or her own.

Results: Engaging in another round of the ongoing cycle

Step 10: Publication
- Each participant, team, or community may prepare a manuscript about the project for publication in a refereed multidisciplinary or disciplinary journal.

Results: Adding to the knowledge base of SoTL

University (CGU) began its Preparing Future Faculty (PFF) program in 2000 with the development of a cohort FLC of graduate students interested in academic careers. It expanded to include a second cohort-based FLC— an advanced graduate student group focused on teaching at liberal arts colleges—and several topic-based FLCs that included both graduate students and faculty members from CGU and faculty from the other Claremont Colleges (Pomona, Scripps, Claremont McKenna, Harvey Mudd, and Pitzer). All FLC participants have the opportunity to attend the regional Lilly Conference on College and University Teaching–West and to present their teaching projects individually or as a group. Graduate students in the two cohort groups prepare full course portfolios in their disciplines, including the design of courses they plan to teach, and write research papers on aspects of the academic career in which they are interested. The 2001–02 group published a fifty-two-page chapter in a textbook on college teaching (Richlin and others, 2002).

Aspects of FLCs That Develop the Scholarship of Teaching and Learning

In order to investigate and confirm what aspects of FLCs develop the scholarship of teaching and learning, it is illuminating to look at the following models. Smith (2001) adapts for SoTL development the Dreyfus and Dreyfus stages of expertise from novice to expert (1986). Applying Smith's adaptation of this model to FLCs (Cox, forthcoming), the stages of development can be described as follows:

Novice: Learns about and uses a few classroom assessment techniques (Angelo and Cross, 1993), checklists, Likert-scale and qualitative surveys to determine effectiveness of FLC project

Advanced beginner: Learns to articulate course learning objectives; recognizes student behaviors or curricular shortcomings that need to change to meet newly articulated objectives

Competent: Chooses areas to investigate; selects or devises ways to assess changes in student behavior or learning objectives in proposed or revised courses; becomes familiar with the literature appropriate to the problem or opportunity for research, then follows procedures

Proficient: Intuitive recognition of problems or opportunities across courses and curricula in the discipline; unless an experienced expert in teaching in the discipline, occurs while member of a subsequent FLC or with an individual research program in SoTL

Expert: Recognizes and researches meta-level disciplinary and transdisciplinary SoTL models, problems, and opportunities

To illustrate one of the stage transitions, the Miami FLC Program provides evidence that repeat FLC participation advances one's expertise. As of 2002–03, out of 950 Miami full-time, tenure-track faculty, 271 (28.5 percent) have participated in an FLC. Of these 271, 81 (30 percent) have participated in an additional FLC. Of these 81 repeaters, 53 percent have reported the production of SoTL with national impact (refereed presentation or publication). Of the 30 who have participated in three or more FLCs, 77 percent have produced national SoTL, and of the 12 who have been in four or five FLCs, 10 (83 percent) have produced national SoTL.

Weston and McAlpine's (2001) developmental three-phase Continuum of Growth Toward SoTL is illuminated and modified by the FLC approach (Cox, forthcoming). In each phase of this model, processes are listed vertically from less complex to more complex. Vertical (within a phase) and lateral (across phases) movement is possible, although "prior to engaging in activities in a subsequent phase, it is necessary to engage in a broad range of activities in the current phase, but not necessarily in all the processes" (Weston and McAlpine, 2001, p. 91). In phase 1, "growth in one's own teaching," a professor develops a personal knowledge of his or her teaching and students' learning, "reducing the conceptual isolation [of SoTL] from the primary scholarly work [scholarship of discovery] of the disciplines and departments" (p. 90). In phase 2, "dialogues with colleagues about teaching and learning," faculty start with conversations in their discipline and move vertically downward to multidisciplinary engagement; "it is necessary to get a sense of community before moving into scholarship" (p. 91), which is phase 3. This phase, "growth in SoTL," covers the same growth as described in the sequence of ten SoTL developmental steps in Miami's FLC Program (Exhibit 11.1).

However, the development toward the scholarship of teaching and learning by faculty in FLCs does not conform to and requires modification of the Weston and McAlpine model, which does not seem to take into account the accelerated development primarily due to the ten steps in the FLC approach to faculty development. Cox (forthcoming) modifies and refines this model based on FLC evidence over the years.

The FLC approach, as analyzed by using these models, provides evidence of the following aspects of FLCs that lead to effective development of the scholarship of teaching and learning:

- Support and safety provided by a community that encourages innovation and risk taking
- A sequence of individual and group developmental steps taken by and shared with the FLC
- The availability of forums for individual and community presentations of project results
- Mentoring of new FLC participants by graduating members
- Transdisciplinarity: multiple perspectives on SoTL
- Reduction of the conceptual isolation of SoTL from discovery scholarship in the disciplines
- Opportunities to repeat the FLC experience in a new FLC

Conclusion

Although more than a decade has passed since the idea of a scholarship of teaching entered the lexicon of American higher education, that concept remains a difficult one to implement. Faculty learning communities provide the teaching scholarship and community support to enable faculty members to become scholars of teaching.

References

Angelo, T. A., and Cross, K. P. *Classroom Assessment Techniques.* San Francisco: Jossey-Bass, 1993.

Boyer, E. L. *Scholarship Reconsidered: Priorities of the Professoriate.* Princeton, N.J.: Carnegie Foundation for the Advancement of Teaching, 1990.

Cox, M. D. "The Development of New and Junior Faculty." In W. A. Wright and Associates (eds.), *Teaching Improvement Practices: Successful Strategies for Higher Education.* Bolton, Mass.: Anker, 1995.

Cox, M. D. "Faculty Learning Communities: Change Agents for Transforming Institutions into Learning Organizations." *To Improve the Academy,* 2001, *19,* 69–93.

Cox, M. D. "Proven Faculty Development Tools That Foster the Scholarship of Teaching in Faculty Learning Communities." *To Improve the Academy,* 2003, *21,* 109–142.

Cox, M. D. "Fostering the Scholarship of Teaching and Learning Through Faculty Learning Communities." Unpublished manuscript, forthcoming.

Cox, M. D. *Faculty Learning Community Program Director's and Facilitator's Handbook:* Oxford, OH: Miami University, 2004.

Dreyfus, H. L., and Dreyfus, S. E. *Mind over Machine: The Power of Human Intuition and Expertise in the Era of the Computer.* New York: Free Press, 1986.

Kreber, C., and Cranton, P. "Exploring the Scholarship of Teaching." *Journal of Higher Education,* forthcoming.

Richlin, L. "The Ongoing Cycle of Scholarly Teaching and the Scholarship of Teaching." Closing plenary presentation at the 13th Annual Lilly Conference on College Teaching, Oxford, Ohio, Nov. 1993a.

Richlin, L. "Openness to a Broader View of Scholarship." In L. Richlin (ed.), *Preparing Faculty for the New Conceptions of Scholarship.* New Directions for Teaching and Learning, no. 54. San Francisco: Jossey-Bass, 1993b.

Richlin, L. "Scholarly Teaching and the 'Scholarship of Teaching': Where Boyer Gets Muddled." Paper presented at the national conference of the Professional and Organizational Development (POD) Network, Snowbird, Utah, Oct. 1998.

Richlin, L. "Scholarly Teaching and the Scholarship of Teaching." In C. Kreber (ed.), *Scholarship Revisited: Perspectives on the Scholarship of Teaching.* New Directions for Teaching and Learning, no. 86. San Francisco: Jossey-Bass, 2001.

Richlin, L., Casad, B. J., Hensley, S., Hilton, J. K., and Williams, J. T. "Teaching and Learning in Different Academic Settings." In G. Wheeler (ed.), *Teaching and Learning in College: A Resource for Educators.* (4th ed.) Elyria, Ohio: Info-Tek, 2002.

Richlin, L., and Cox, M. D. "Enhancing Faculty Publishing Opportunities Through Understanding the Criteria and Standards for the Scholarship of Teaching." Paper presented at the Politics and Processes of Scholarly Publishing conference, University of South Florida, St. Petersburg, Mar. 12, 1994.

Smith, R. "Expertise and the Scholarship of Teaching." In C. Kreber (ed.), *Scholarship Revisited: Perspectives on the Scholarship of Teaching.* New Directions for Teaching and Learning, no. 86. San Francisco: Jossey-Bass, 2001.

Weston, C. B., and McAlpine, L. "Making Explicit the Development Toward the Scholarship of Teaching." In C. Kreber (ed.), *Scholarship Revisited: Perspectives on the Scholarship of Teaching.* New Directions for Teaching and Learning, no. 86. San Francisco: Jossey-Bass, 2001.

LAURIE RICHLIN is director of the Preparing Future Faculty and faculty learning communities programs at Claremont Graduate University and director of the Lilly Conference on College and University Teaching–West.

MILTON D. COX is director of the Center for the Enhancement of Learning and Teaching at Miami University, where he founded and directs the Lilly Conference on College Teaching and facilitates the Hesburgh Award–winning Teaching Scholars Faculty Learning Community.

Faculty members' productivity may shift over time, not as a function of age but as a function of the amount of time a senior faculty member spends with colleagues (Bland and Bergquist, 1997). This chapter shows how faculty learning communities can provide the opportunities and connections that senior and midcareer faculty need to continue productive academic lives.

Midcareer and Senior Faculty Learning Communities: Learning Throughout Faculty Careers

Muriel L. Blaisdell, Milton D. Cox

> There is . . . nothing intrinsically wrong with processed information, but there is something wrong with a society that spends so much money—as well as countless hours of human effort—to make the least dregs of processed information available to everyone everywhere and yet does little or nothing to help us explore the world for ourselves.
> —Edward S. Reed (1996, p. 3)

The epigram that begins this essay is a quotation from Edward S. Reed's book *The Necessity of Experience*. He advocates a shift in educational practice from mainstream practice, which emphasizes learning from books and "processed information," to learning from experience. People tend to confront the dilemma of rigor or relevance—whether to choose the high ground of research-based theory or the swampy lowlands, where problems are messy and confusing—when they reach the age of about 45. At this point they ask themselves, 'Am I going to do the thing I was trained for, on which I base my claims to technical rigor and academic respectability? Or am I going to work on the problems—ill formed, vague, and messy—that I have discovered to be real around here?'" (Schön, 1995, p. 28). This dilemma closely parallels our experience in working with midcareer and senior faculty development. As teachers and scholars, we are adept at learning from reading, computers, lectures, and other forms of processed knowledge. But we are coming to value direct experience more and more as a complement to familiar processed learning formats.

Faculty development for midcareer and late-career faculty members is more analogous to in-service learning or continuing education than to revitalization, a word that suggests that vitality is at an ebb or even totally absent. It is essential to begin with the realistic view that faculty will have a variety of needs, including rethinking their teaching, trying new pedagogies, and even general inspiration, but it is equally essential not to begin with a negative assessment of the cohort one serves as somehow lacking, deficient, or not fully vital. McMahan and Plank (2003) call their paper about their midcareer and senior faculty program at The Ohio State University "Old Dogs Teaching Each Other New Tricks." "Old dogs" have been learning every day of their careers. As leaders and mentors of younger faculty in the university, senior and midcareer faculty are experiencing the need to shift paradigms from one that emphasizes knowledge, teaching techniques, and testing to a new focus on student learning and outcomes assessment (Barr and Tagg, 1995). Most senior faculty apply for a senior faculty learning community (SFLC) not because their teaching needs to be fired up but because they wish to take their work in new directions and because they long for sharing with new discussion partners.

Senior Faculty

Rice and Finkelstein (1993) portrayed senior faculty who joined the professoriate between 1965 and 1974, a time of expansion and optimism, as living through a significant downturn in higher education that dampened individual and generational expectations. Confident that teaching would play a key role in effecting change in academe and society, they saw research, publication, and grant acquisition come to be valued over teaching and institutional citizenship (Rice, 1980). As new faculty members embraced different priorities and rewards, some seniors found themselves out of step with their institution and their discipline. In a study of 111 senior faculty on eleven New Jersey campuses, LaCelle-Peterson and Finkelstein (1993) found that senior faculty care a great deal about teaching but find little opportunity to focus on it; collegial interaction is limited and departmental discussion of teaching is scarce, a finding that is confirmed in a study by Massy, Wilger, and Colbeck (1994). Boice (1993), in interviews with fifty department chairs who were dealing with 919 disillusioned faculty members at a research institution and a comprehensive institution, found that one third of the disillusioned faculty members were socially isolated from their colleagues and were frequent sources of student complaints. They attributed their disillusionment partly to their isolation from colleagues and students. Karpiak (1997) created a schema that represents midcareer faculty members' feelings about their career as university faculty. These feelings range from low interest marked by malaise and not mattering, which she called marginality, to high interest and mattering, in which one's work offers meaning and the sense that one's achievements matter not only to the faculty member but also to the wider community. One lesson for the faculty developer is that these designations are not permanent features of a faculty member's life or character but are labile if university support is available to facilitate shifts from the low side of malaise and marginality toward the high side of meaning and mattering.

In the eleven years that Muriel Blaisdell served as facilitator of the Senior Faculty Learning Community for Teaching Excellence at Miami University (MU), she found the age status of the members of the community to be relevant in a way that is not always discussed. More experienced teachers are often seeking an open door to other faculty from different departments or who have very different approaches to teaching. They are ready to let new people know and see what they are doing in class. The fresh social and intellectual mix of people in the SFLC is one of its most desirable features. Even if people join the group looking for an opportunity to do a particular teaching-related project, the group itself usually ends up being a more memorable and important aspect of the experience (Table 12.1). The more senior a faculty member is, the greater the need for recognition of excellence in efforts and achievements in teaching that leads to student learning. Being chosen for membership in an SFLC is an award, not a development experience. The group is made up of people who join a kind of "intentional community."

Faculty members are eligible to participate in the SFLC if they are full-time with tenure and seven years of teaching experience at MU. As a consequence of this broad definition, associate professors and full professors work together in the community. In the eleven years of the SFLC, there have been ninety participants: thirty-nine full professors, forty-eight associate professors, one assistant professor, and one senior instructor (plus one record missing). Participants in one SFLC may also represent two generations—the eldest members of the group may have children about the ages of the youngest members. Even by the first five years of the SRLC, members' years of experience at MU ranged through every number between eight and twenty-nine. Sixteen years of experience at MU is both the mean and the median of participants. There is diversity not only in age and experience but also in departmental affiliation and leadership. Over the eleven years of the SFLC at MU, membership has come from 75 percent (33 of 44) of the academic departments, all six divisions, and all three campuses. Two participants were department chairs while members of the SFLC, nine had previously been chairs, and two became chairs in a future year. Members may be teaching in lecture halls, in seminars, in one-on-one tutorials or lessons, or via distance learning. The use of technology may also vary enormously. Faculty members come to the SFLC for many different reasons, and the community must make that diversity into an asset; almost always, it succeeds.

Table 12.1. Miami University and The Ohio State University Assessment of Faculty Learning Community Components

Results for the following question:
"Estimate the impact of the community on you with respect to each of the following program components. '1' indicates a very weak impact, and '10' indicates a very strong impact."

Component (listed in order of impact across all FLCs)	MU Junior Faculty FLC (20 years)	MU Senior and Mid Faculty FLC (10 years)	OSU Junior Faculty FLC (1 year)	OSU Senior and Mid Faculty FLC (1 year)
1. The colleagueship and learning from other participants	(1) 8.9	(2) 8.7	(4) 7.7	(1) 10.0
2. The retreats and conferences	(2) 8.3	(3) 7.8	(1) 9.0	(7) 8.3
3. Release time (Junior, Senior, MU) or funds for professional expenses (MU and OSU)	(3) 8.1	(1) 8.8	(4) 7.7	(6) 8.8
4. The teaching project	(4) 8.0	(5) 7.7	(3) 8.0	(5) 9.2
5. Seminars	(6) 7.7	(6) 7.5	(7) 7.0	(1) 10.0
6. Student associates	(7) 5.8	(3) 7.8	—	—
7. A one-to-one faculty partnership (Junior at MU and OSU: experienced faculty mentor; Senior at MU: faculty partners in learning)	(5) 7.9	(8) 5.9	(8) 6.5	—
8. Observation of a faculty partner's and others' classes	(8) 6.8	(7) 6.2	—	—
9. Consult with faculty and TA development staff	—	—	(2) 8.7	(1) 10.0
10. Faculty and TA development programs	—	—	(4) 7.7	(4) 9.3
Overall Mean for Cohort	7.7	7.6	7.8	9.4

Notes:

FLC = Faculty learning community.

MU = Miami University.

OSU = The Ohio State University.

This table includes reports from those who engaged in a particular component and rated it.

In column headings, number of years in parentheses indicates number of years surveyed.

In table body, the number in parentheses is the overall ranking of the component for all the years in which the question has been asked.

In table body, the other number is the mean for the component for all the years in which the question has been asked.

Each SFLC member at MU receives one-course release time for one semester and $500 for expenses related to his or her teaching project. This provides time for necessary reflection and sends the message that the university values their contribution.

At MU, we reviewed application and evaluation materials to answer the question "Why do senior faculty step forward to participate in FLCs?" We identified some widely shared concerns among these senior faculty (Cox and Blaisdell, 1995):

Resolving long-term problems: "After twenty years I still struggle with grading. . . ."

Need for "intersubjective verification": "I thought that [issue x] was just a problem in science teaching, but you have the same problem in art."

Need for new sociointellectual stimuli: "After twenty years in my department, I need some new people to talk with who don't know or care about the politics of my department."

Previous good faculty development experience: "I learned a lot in the program for junior faculty." (One third of the SFLC members were previously in the junior faculty FLC.)

Interdisciplinary interests: "I'd like to bring some social issues into my genetics class and am glad for a climate that promotes that kind of growth."

Different faculty and student expectations: "I love my field, but students see it only as a requirement and don't come to love the calculus."

Responses to student criticism: "I've tried all kinds of things, but I can't seem to get good student evaluations."

Issues related to diversity: "I wonder if my classroom is 'chilly' to anyone." "Could my curriculum be more inclusive?"

Responding to changes in students: "I feel like there has been a decline in student preparation [or motivation, or particular skills], and I'm not sure how to respond."

Responding to technological changes: "Nothing in grad school prepared me for this technology [or curriculum, or pedagogy, or student population]."

Achievements and projects: "I've wanted to work on this course idea for years and haven't had a chance." "At last I can try multimedia authoring."

Longing for time to reflect: "The release time is a big help in getting some reading done, and it gives me a chance to think."

Faculty members have greatly varying teaching loads, from one or two courses in a semester to four, and most have significant service involvement as well as student advising and research projects. Some people have contact with a few students, and others have hundreds. Leaves for research go some way to offer renewal to faculty but are too rare to fully satisfy the need for continuing education as a scholarly teacher, to say nothing of the desire many faculty members have to participate in the scholarship of teaching and learning. Full professors may feel greater freedom to publish articles on

Table 12.2. Comparisons of Miami University Junior and Senior Faculty in Their FLCs

Junior Faculty*	Senior Faculty**
Behavior at End of a Typical Seminar	
Busy, off to next activity, or, late in the day, to family right at end of seminar	Relaxed, wanting to sit and discuss items after time to adjourn
Attendance at Off-Campus Retreats	
Everyone comes, stays entire time	Some (20–25%) cannot come due to conflicts; some drop in for part
Attendance at a National Conference	
All go, travel together	Sometimes members split up and attend different conferences, then share with the FLC on return
Interaction	
Collaborative, cooperative; enjoy each other	Autonomous; some find it difficult to cooperate
Common Causes	
Rally around newness, tenure	Share individual views: administration, university politics, promotion concerns
Teaching	
Enthusiastic, upbeat, curious: willing to experiment	Some cautious, careful, skeptical; some hesitant to experiment at first
Most participants are or become "quick starters" (Boice, 1992)	

*Alumni Teaching Scholars Community for Junior Faculty (25 years)

**Senior Faculty Learning Community for Teaching Excellence (11 years)

Source: Adapted from Cox and Blaisdell, 1995.

teaching outside their research areas than assistant and associate professors may feel. Table 12.2 indicates other differences in the behaviors of junior and senior faculty in the FLCs that we have facilitated at MU over the years.

The SFLC seems to succeed because the activities of the group are multidimensional. There are a variety of people to work with—new colleagues, new disciplinary associations, student associates—plus readings in student development and faculty development literature, as well as the opportunity to work on teaching projects.

Senior Faculty *Learning*

Why do I teach? Why do you? What are your greatest challenges in motivating your students? What strategies do you find most effective? How can active learning be achieved in large lecture classes? Which sessions of the conference on college teaching gave you an idea you would like to try in your classes? These are the kinds of issues we discuss during the informal portion of our meetings, which will often feature discussion of a reading, a guest presentation, or a presentation by a member of the group. Palmer (1976) called such meaningful encounters "meetings for learning."

Learning is a major part of what faculty and students share, and it is a shared activity through which community between them may be constructed. It must be remembered that as teaching experience increases, so does the distance from graduate training and postdoctoral research fellowships. Senior faculty have learned new fields and followed the remaking of their discipline as knowledge has increased and changed. The university benefits from supporting this transformation in both research fields and in teaching. Many senior faculty come to realize that they can benefit from knowing how other faculty members handle the necessity of reinventing their knowledge base and their methods of teaching that knowledge.

One method of nurturing this learning exchange is to set up pairings of people from widely disparate areas. Joseph Katz and Mildred Henry (1988), in their book *Turning Professors into Teachers: A New Approach to Faculty Development and Student Learning,* described their plan for such cross-disciplinary exchanges. The state of New Jersey adopted their design and called it "Partners in Learning" (Smith and Smith, 1993). Implementing a version of this plan keeps the focus on student learning by involving pairs of faculty in visiting each other's classes and in interviewing the other person's students. Not only does it serve the person who is seeking to improve the course being studied, but it also serves the visiting faculty member, granting access through the interviews to students who are learning in a different subject or methodological field.

At MU, each member of the SFLC chooses a student associate who works on projects with the faculty member and who is invited to attend selected SFLC meetings. Discussions at those meetings will often consider student concerns about grading, workload, or course development. Meetings with students generally include creative activities such as devising analogies that best describe teaching and learning. In this informal setting, students feel free to ask questions about faculty life and to share the joys and stresses they experience in their lives as students. A seminar at which faculty and students share their views of teaching and learning is a highlight of the year (Cox and Sorenson, 1999).

In the SFLC, we have found that meeting for learning off campus as well as on campus is an important element of our program. Retreats give us extended time together, allowing ideas to emerge. We travel to attend conferences and often to give papers on teaching-related research. These opportunities for extended time together are particularly instrumental in developing the cohesive feeling of community in each year's group. SFLC members have appreciated attending the meetings of the Association of American Colleges and Universities and the American Association for Higher Education. Educational policy, the future of academic institutions, and new directions in higher education are subjects of greater interest to senior faculty than to those just out of graduate school. Members may have chaired universitywide committees or served on the Liberal Education Council, the University Senate, or other bodies that have made them aware of and interested in how MU is situated in American higher education. At national conferences, they may attend a session on how universities are facing up to the challenges of alcohol on their campuses or strategies for increasing diversity.

Each fall begins with a discussion of a focus book that is selected by the facilitator and presented to new participants at the opening retreat in the spring. Four books that have worked well for establishing conversations that last all year are *Embracing Contraries* (Elbow, 1986), *When Hope and Fear Collide* (Levine and Cureton, 1998), *Making Their Own Way* (Baxter Magolda, 2001), and *The Courage to Teach.* (Palmer, 1998). Through readings and discussions, senior faculty begin to see how they can bring to their learning about teaching the intellectual rigor and depth that they apply in their discovery research. We have seen that there is a need to make senior faculty aware of events and programs that may be new to them or that may have changed in the last few years. We invite guests to our meetings who have special knowledge of new data on student development, managing learning disabilities or mental health issues, recent initiatives to improve student and faculty diversity, service learning, or whatever the group is curious to learn. Focus books and the ensuing discussions are an important part of the sequence of developmental steps that lead to participants' production of the scholarship of teaching and learning (Cox, 2003).

In FLCs, opportunities are offered to learn from discussing issues with other faculty members, from doing projects, and from working with students. We cast our nets broadly in a search for knowledge and for projects that we can do together. We are increasingly collaborative and constructive in our collective learning style. One characteristic of the senior faculty development experience is that it is usually the teachers who are already very good who are most eager for opportunities to advance their creative and explorative talents even further, so the group develops a positive momentum as members inspire each other.

Senior Faculty Learning *Community*

Ernest Boyer, in his foreword to the Carnegie Foundation's (1990) report *Campus Life: In Search of Community,* described the general need in American higher education for renewal. He organized his findings under six distinct expressions of community: purposeful, open, just, disciplined, caring, and celebrative. Creating FLCs as a part of a faculty development program has helped MU to give form to the *Campus Life* ideals. In the SFLC, we have made a real effort to express our aspirations for excellence in college teaching in a purposeful way and to be affirming of diverse people and teaching issues. We do our best to be just in selecting each group and in providing a supportive and challenging environment in which good work thrives. It is in the caring and celebrative aspects of community that some of the greatest gains for senior faculty occur. A blend of intense and measurable work and hospitality is needed and appreciated by senior faculty, who are often underappreciated in their departments.

We recognize that the eight to eleven faculty members in our SFLC come from a wide variety of disciplines. If there is to be a sense of unity in the group it must come from a sense of common purpose and meaning that is generated at a level different from our academic fields. Fortunately, every group has the potential to feel that it is a uniquely compatible group. Varied academic interests and areas of specialization strengthen the group. One person's perspective provides continuing education for another individual, who may never have talked at length with an engineer in paper science or with someone who plays the oboe. That kind of interaction, friendship, and informal learning has a substantive impact on a senior teacher's interactions with students and particularly on advising that is difficult to measure. An SFLC member knows someone who is easy to call with a question about courses and curricula quite different from his or her own. The experience of being in a faculty community leads to a strong sense of universitywide citizenship that is important for morale as well as for working with students.

We like to say, "The 'C' is the key to the FLC!" Community is one of the special gifts that FLCs give to their participants and to the wider communities of which the members are a part. Even when an individual is working alone on a teaching project, the community benefits. A course or set of courses may be transformed, a new computer skill may be mastered, or an experimental pedagogy might be created. Financial support of up to $500 is available to each member for the individual project. At the end of the academic year, there will be a universitywide seminar to share achievements of individuals and of the group as a whole. The closing SFLC retreat will be a forum in which the "graduates" will share their projects with the incoming group. The retreat is characterized by the strong desire of the SFLC that is ending its year to convey to the new SFLC how much they have learned from the chance to be together.

Other Midcareer and Senior FLCs

Two FLCs that differ from the MU model mix senior and junior faculty and have been in existence for several years. The President's Teaching Scholars Program was established at the University of Colorado in 1989 to honor and reward faculty for exemplary teaching and scholarship. Members of the President's Teaching Scholars FLC serve as ambassadors for teaching and research. They establish and develop individual, departmental, and campuswide projects, including mentoring, that are aimed at the cultivation of teaching and engaged learning as well as the integration of research in teaching at the university. "Over time, we have found that this group is composed of members who enjoy the opportunity to interact, engage and grow with colleagues whose values, generosity of spirit and concerns about education are shared" (http://www.colorado.edu/UCB/ptsp/call.html). Those appointed as teaching scholars receive a $3,000 stipend for each of the first two years; a one-time teaching development fund of $2,000; and an addition of $2,000 to their base salary beginning in the third year.

In 1988, a Fund for the Improvement of Post-Secondary Education (FIPSE) grant funded the first three years of the Senior Teaching Fellows Program at the University of Georgia (UG). This yearlong program engages eight senior faculty (associate or full professors who have been at UG for at least five years) in a variety of activities that include development of a teaching project in a focus course, mentoring teaching assistants or junior faculty who are teaching that course, seminars and retreats on teaching and learning, and consultation with the university president (Kalivoda, Broder, and Jackson, 2003). Each fellow receives $2,500 for the project. For success, "the keys are thoughtful planning, developing trust and esprit de corps, strong staff support, and strong leadership from faculty members who participate" (Jackson and Simpson, 1993, p. 78).

Of the sixty FLCs initiated by the five adapting institutions in the MU FIPSE FLC project (see Chapter One), only The Ohio State University started a midcareer and senior faculty program, an FLC for tenured faculty. Initiated in 2002–03, the FLC consisted of eight faculty members selected from thirty-five applicants. Each received $750, with the possibility of matching funds from the participant's department and college. They met monthly, usually during dinner, with everyone contributing toward the purchase of food. Agenda topics during the first few meetings were determined by the facilitator and later by the discussion that developed at the previous meeting. Assessment results are shown in Table 12.1. Participants felt that teaching development for posttenure faculty was important because of the push to have experienced faculty teach introductory courses, a widening generation gap (faculty age increases, but students are mostly the same age every year), and the ripple effect that dissemination will have on search committees, mentoring, and colleagues (McMahan and Plank, 2003).

Conclusion

Leaders of SFLCs may find the concept of servant leadership associated with the work of Greenleaf (Senge, 1995) and others worth considering. Senior faculty are very astute in knowing their own needs and in leading the activities they choose. The faculty developer's role is chiefly to serve as a facilitator of that process. Faculty development for senior faculty may also involve keeping the focus on translating the work we do together as faculty members into meaningful change in student learning and in making the climate for teaching and learning in the university as creative and diverse as it can be. Boyer (Carnegie Foundation, 1990, p. 16) states:

We conclude that the quality of a college or university must be measured first by the commitment of its members to the *educational* mission of the institution. It is in the classroom where community begins, but learning also reaches out to departments, to residential halls, to the campus commons. The curriculum, too, if properly designed, should intellectually integrate the campus. In a *purposeful* community, learning is pervasive.

The maturity and determination to continue to learn throughout their career that we have seen in the senior faculty is an asset to the university. The choice to join a senior faculty learning community dedicated to teaching excellence and engaging other colleagues, to invest time in improving learning in students and faculty, is an act of generosity and should be treated by the university as a sign, as Karpiak (1997) wrote, of high "interest and caring" as well as a deterrent to feelings of malaise and marginality.

References

Barr, R. B., and Tagg, J. "From Teaching to Learning—A New Paradigm for Undergraduate Education." *Change*, Nov.–Dec. 1995, pp. 13–25.

Baxter Magolda, M. B. *Making Their Own Way: Narratives for Transforming Higher Education to Promote Self-Development.* Sterling, Va.: Stylus, 2001.

Bland, C. J., and Bergquist, W. H. *The Vitality of Senior Faculty Members: Snow on the Roof—Fire in the Furnace.* ASHE-ERIC Higher Education Report, vol. 25, no. 7. Washington, D.C.: Graduate School of Education and Human Development, George Washington University, 1997.

Boice, R. *The New Faculty Member: Supporting and Fostering Professional Development.* San Francisco: Jossey-Bass, 1992.

Boice, R. "Primal Origins and Later Correctives for Midcareer Disillusionment." In M. J. Finkelstein and M. W. LaCelle-Peterson (eds.), *Developing Senior Faculty as Teachers.* New Directions for Teaching and Learning, no. 55. San Francisco: Jossey-Bass, 1993.

Carnegie Foundation for the Advancement of Teaching. *Campus Life: In Search of Community.* (Foreword by E. Boyer). Princeton: Princeton University Press, 1990.

Cox, M. D. "Proven Faculty Development Tools That Foster the Scholarship of Teaching in Faculty Learning Communities." *To Improve the Academy*, 2003, 21, 109–142.

Cox, M. D., and Blaisdell, M. "Teaching Development for Senior Faculty: Searching for Fresh Solutions in a Salty Sea." Paper presented at the 20th annual conference of the Professional and Organizational Development Network in Higher Education, North Falmouth, Mass., Oct. 1995.

Cox, M. D., and Sorenson, D. L. "Student Collaboration in Faculty Development: Connecting Directly to the Learning Revolution." *To Improve the Academy*, 1999, 18, 97–127.

Elbow, P. *Embracing Contraries: Explorations in Learning and Teaching.* New York: Oxford University Press, 1986.

Greenleaf, R. K. *Servant Leadership. A Journey into the Nature of Legitimate Power and Greatness.* New York: Paulist Press, 1977.

Jackson, W. K., and Simpson, R. D. "Redefining the Role of Senior Faculty at a Research University." In M. J. Finkelstein and M. W. LaCelle-Peterson (eds.), *Developing Senior Faculty as Teachers.* New Directions for Teaching and Learning, no. 55. San Francisco: Jossey-Bass, 1993.

Kalivoda, P., Broder, J., and Jackson, W. K. "Establishing a Teaching Academy: Cultivation of Teaching at a Research University Campus." *To Improve the Academy*, 2003, *21*, 79–92.

Karpiak, I. E. "University Professors at Mid-Life: Being a Part of. . . . but Feeling Apart." *To Improve the Academy*, 1997, *16*, 21–40.

Katz, J., and Henry, M. *Turning Professors into Teachers: A New Approach to Faculty Development and Student Learning*. New York: American Council on Education and Macmillan, 1988.

LaCelle-Peterson, M. W., and Finkelstein, M. J. "Institutions Matter: Campus Teaching Environments' Impact on Senior Faculty." In M. J. Finkelstein and M. W. LaCelle-Peterson (eds.), *Developing Senior Faculty as Teachers*. New Directions for Teaching and Learning, no. 55. San Francisco: Jossey-Bass, 1993.

Levine, A., and Cureton, J. S. *When Hope and Fear Collide: A Portrait of Today's College Student*. San Francisco: Jossey-Bass, 1998.

Massy, W. F., Wilger, A. K., and Colbeck, C. "Overcoming 'Hollowed' Collegiality: Departmental Cultures and Teaching Quality." *Change*, July–Aug. 1994, pp. 11–20.

McMahan, M., and Plank, K. M. "Old Dogs Teaching Each Other New Tricks: Learning Communities for Post-Tenure Faculty." Paper presented at the 23rd annual Lilly Conference on College Teaching, Miami University, Oxford, Ohio, Nov. 2003.

Palmer, P. J. *Meeting for Learning: Education in a Quaker Context*. Pamphlet no. 284. Wallingford, Penn.: Pendle Hill, 1976.

Palmer, P. J. *The Courage to Teach: Exploring the Inner Landscape of a Teacher's Life*. San Francisco: Jossey-Bass, 1998.

Reed, E. S. *The Necessity of Experience*. New Haven, Conn.: Yale University Press, 1996.

Rice, R. E. "Dreams and Actualities: Danforth Fellows in Mid-Career." *AAHE Bulletin*, 1980, *32*(8), 3–16.

Rice, R. E., and Finkelstein, M. J. "The Senior Faculty: A Portrait and Literature Review." In M. J. Finkelstein and M. W. LaCelle-Peterson (eds.), *Developing Senior Faculty as Teachers*. New Directions for Teaching and Learning, no. 55. San Francisco: Jossey-Bass, 1993.

Schön, D. A. "The New Scholarship Requires a New Epistemology." *Change*, 1995, *27*(6), pp. 27–34.

Senge, P. M. "Robert Greenleaf's Legacy: A New Foundation for Twenty-First Century Institutions." In L. C. Spears (ed.), *Reflections on Leadership: How Robert K. Greenleaf's Theory of Servant-Leadership Influenced Today's Top Management Thinkers*. New York: Wiley, 1995.

Smith, B. L., and Smith, M. J. "Revitalizing Senior Faculty Through Statewide Efforts." In M. J. Finkelsteinand M. W. LaCelle-Peterson (eds.), *Developing Senior Faculty as Teachers*. New Directions for Teaching and Learning, no. 55. San Francisco: Jossey-Bass, 1993.

MURIEL L. BLAISDELL *is professor of interdisciplinary studies at Miami University in Oxford, Ohio. She is founder of the Senior Faculty Learning Community for Teaching Excellence, which she facilitated for eleven years.*

MILTON D. COX *is director of the Center for the Enhancement of Scholarship and Teaching at Miami University, where he has served as FLC program director and consultant to the Senior Faculty Community for Teaching Excellence during its eleven years. He has also facilitated the junior faculty FLC for twenty-five years.*

Faculty learning communities have many attributes
that can contribute to the successful preparation of
graduate students as future faculty members.

Faculty Learning Communities for Preparing Future Faculty

Laurie Richlin, Amy Essington

Doctoral programs are designed to prepare students to be competent researchers. However, the majority of faculty members (93.8 percent) work in nondoctoral institutions in which the majority of their time is spent teaching (National Study of Postsecondary Faculty, 1999). Hiring institutions have claimed that candidates often do not show expertise in teaching or an understanding of their institution's culture and students (Richlin, 1991). Until programs addressed this issue, the training of doctoral students was focused on research, without the elements of teaching and service that also will play an important role in their academic career. To address the reality of doctoral students who become academics and will spend much of their career in classrooms, programs have been developed to prepare future faculty for teaching and other issues of academic life.

In 1993, the Council of Graduate Schools (CGS) and the Association of American Colleges and Universities (AAC&U) developed a joint initiative to improve the preparation of graduate students for faculty roles. Funded by the Pew Charitable Trusts, the National Science Foundation, and an anonymous donor, CGS/AAC&U Preparing Future Faculty (PFF) programs address issues not covered in most graduate programs. PFF programs include three core features: gaining teaching experience; learning about the academic triad of research, teaching, and service; and mentoring (Preparing Future Faculty National Office, n.d., p. 3). The ultimate goal of the program is to prepare alumni for success as assistant professors. In addition to those working in the CGS/AAC&U program, some institutions have developed

PFF programs on their own, and some have developed programs that use elements of the CGS/AAC&U model.

The CGS/AAC&U program has involved forty-three doctoral institutions and a total of 295 institutions in collaborative clusters for graduate student teaching experiences. The program developed in four phases. In the first phase, five doctoral-producing institutions received substantial grants to establish extended PFF programs, and twelve institutions received similar grants to start smaller PFF programs. The second phase included ten of the institutions from the first phase and five new institutions with PFF-like activities. During this phase, the pilot PFF programs were institutionalized. The National Science Foundation supported nineteen institutions in developing PFF programs for math and science graduate students during the third phase. During the fourth and final phase, six disciplinary societies supported PFF development programs for graduate students in the humanities and social sciences.

The CGS/AAC&U program has three core features: a cluster of a doctoral institution and partner institutions that provide training situations; activities to help students understand the triad of academic life; and mentoring. From acquiring teaching experience to observing faculty committees to working with a teaching mentor, PFF participants are exposed to multiple layers of life in academia. The partner institutions offer students from the graduate institution opportunities to teach and participate in roles and responsibilities on their campuses. Participation in a range of activities related to academic life leads to examination of aspects of life on different campuses. Multiple mentors round out the experience and support the doctoral students (Preparing Future Faculty National Office, n.d., p. 4).

Other institutions have taken on elements of the national PFF program and made PFF fit their own needs, creating what AAC&U calls campuswide versions, department-based versions, institutions with PFF elements, and miscellaneous versions.

What Is Really Needed

As Cox reports in Chapter One of this volume, Rice, Sorcinelli, and Austin (2000) identified three core concerns of future and early-career faculty as lack of a comprehensible tenure system, lack of community, and lack of integration of their academic and personal lives. One graduate student in the *Heeding New Voices* study stated, "What I want most in a faculty career is a profession that makes me feel connected to my students, to my colleagues, to the larger community, and to myself" (p. 13). Programs to prepare future faculty need to include elements that address these concerns. Foremost is developing wisdom about the academic process so that in selecting an institution, future faculty members can find the best fit for their interests and can negotiate the tenure process successfully. Community, as Cox noted in Chapter One, is an important element for all graduate education because lack of community is one of four reasons that students leave graduate school that were identified by Lovitts (2001). (The others are lack of information about doctoral study and ability to navigate the system, disappointment with the learning experience, and an unsatisfactory adviser relationship.) Finally, PFF programs should model the integration of study, teaching, and service with personal, family, and public life.

The Faculty Learning Community Model for PFF

Faculty learning communities provide an ideal model of what an academic career should be like. In faculty learning communities (FLCs), colleagues from across disciplines meet with enough regularity to develop both intellectual and personal trust. Many FLC social activities include families. Seminar discussions focus on all aspects of academic life, including teaching, research, and institutional service. New resources (for example, conferences, books, etc.) are provided both by and to the participants so that they can reflect on their work, broaden their understanding of faculty life, and meet their career goals. FLCs also can provide documentation of future faculty members' work on teaching and their understanding of academic responsibilities through course portfolios or teaching portfolios and academic credit.

A PFF FLC is unique because its participants are part of two communities: the institution in which they are getting their degree and the institution in which they are teaching. As part-time instructors where they teach, doctoral students participate, in a limited way, in the world of academia. They gain experience in another institutional setting and culture and learn to take responsibility for planning and conducting courses for students who are different from the ones at their doctoral institution. Unlike a new full-time faculty member at the institution where they are teaching, graduate students in a PFF FLC are able to return to a welcoming FLC of peers at their home institution to process and analyze both their positive and negative teaching experiences. By structuring the PFF program as an FLC, the elements of an FLC that build community, such as social activities, help to create a strong network in which students can learn in a safe environment about teaching, academic life, and faculty roles and responsibilities.

PFF Faculty Learning Communities

The survey reported in Chapter Two found fifteen FLCs for graduate student cohorts: thirteen FLCs at eleven U.S. doctoral/research universities and two at Canadian universities. Six of the eleven U.S. institutions that reported using the FLC format for their PFF programs did not receive funding from the national program coordinated by CGS/AAC&U. The format varies among the campuses. The University of New Hampshire has two programs, one campuswide and the other in the psychology department. These programs have been supported by FIPSE grants. Michigan State University also has two programs, one in the College of Natural Science and another that operates across several colleges. Virginia Commonwealth University's PFF program is designed specifically to prepare faculty in the professions. Their program also was developed with a FIPSE grant. Kent State University includes both faculty members and future faculty members in their PFF cohort. The Ohio State University does not classify its Graduate Teaching Fellows FLC program as a PFF program; the graduate student participants are chosen from each department and are responsible for designing a teaching improvement program project to take back to the graduate students in their departments. Mount Royal College uses graduate student triads in their FLC, to encourage peer collaboration. Miami University's campuswide program evolved from the CGS/AAC&U-supported PFF program in Miami's psychology department; participants teach or intern on a Miami University regional campus. The University of Texas–El Paso has more than fifteen graduate students in its PFF FLC, who meet every two weeks during the fall term. As described below, with support from the Miami University FIPSE grant, Claremont Graduate University (CGU) has expanded its PFF FLC program to include graduate students in topic-based communities as well as cohort FLCs.

The Claremont Graduate University PFF FLC Adaptation

CGU PFF program activities have three goals: prepare students for an academic career, prepare students to teach at a variety of institutions, and prepare students to be outstanding researchers of the twenty-first century. CGU is a freestanding graduate school, part of The Claremont Consortium, which also includes Pomona, Scripps, Claremont McKenna, Harvey Mudd, and Pitzer colleges. Those elite undergraduate schools pride themselves on having small classes taught by their professors, not teaching assistants. Because of this, CGU students do not have the support and opportunities that students in traditional universities acquire through teaching assistantships. On the other hand, CGU is located in Southern California in the midst of over three hundred community, state, and private colleges and universities, where CGU students can (and do) find adjunct positions.

The Preparing Future Faculty program at CGU comprises a multilevel set of experiences for students in all disciplines and programs. Primary activities are designed as part of faculty learning communities.

FLCs Open to Faculty Members and CGU Students

Several of the programs include both CGU students and faculty members from CGU and the other Claremont Colleges.

Professional Development Practicum. The Professional Development Practicum is an informal community with a series of twelve workshops (six per semester) that are open to all members of the CGU community. Workshops focus on the academic career, teaching, and research preparation. Participants who complete ten of the twelve workshops receive a certificate from the provost.

Topic-Based FLCs. During 2003–04, there are two topic-based FLCs of ten to fifteen members each that include full-time faculty and professional staff from all of The Claremont Colleges and CGU students who meet the criteria specified for each community. Different FLC topics are selected each year, although it is possible to form new groups on the same or similar topics. Previous years' topics include Teaching Writing-Enriched Courses, the Psychology of Learning, and Teaching with Technology.

FLC on Teaching Women's Studies Courses. This FLC emphasizes feminist scholarship and methodologies, based on the premise that gender is significant in social, cultural, and scientific study. It includes seven faculty members from multiple disciplines at The Claremont Colleges who are designing or updating a women's study course. This FLC also includes seven CGU graduate students.

FLC on Teaching Research Methods Across the Curriculum. This FLC brings together faculty members from multiple disciplines at The Claremont Colleges and graduate students who teach research methods or who assign research projects in their courses to investigate common goals, challenges, and strategies. The FLC uses information literacy as a framework for identifying and discussing how the growth of information affects students' ability to conduct research in their disciplines. There are fourteen members: eleven graduate students and three professional staff or faculty members.

FLCs Open Only to CGU Students

Two FLCs are designed only for CGU students interested in pursuing an academic career.

FLC on Preparing Future Faculty. Fellows in CGU's Preparing Future Faculty Program participate in a yearlong learning community, which includes a weekly seminar and a set of experiences designed to introduce them to some of the many issues that surround a career in higher education. Each fellow has a faculty mentor from CGU or an institution where they teach. There are sixteen students participating in the 2003–04 PFF Fellows FLC. In the fall the fellows participate in the Seminar on the Academic Profession, which studies issues that relate to a faculty career in higher education, such as the various institutional contexts in American higher education, issues that face new faculty members in their first academic job, and resources that will help them succeed in their first faculty position. In the spring they take the Teaching and Learning in Higher Education seminar, which addresses issues of teaching and student learning, including understanding student diversity and learning styles.

During the year, fellows construct a full course portfolio for an introductory course in their discipline.

FLC on Professional Teaching and Training. The Professional Teaching and Training Program (PTTP) Scholars FLC prepares up to twelve advanced graduate students each year to be liberal arts college teachers. Scholars participate in a weekly graduate seminar during the training year, followed by a one-semester internship the next academic year. Through a grant from the JL Foundation, PTTP scholars receive a $1,750 stipend each semester during the first year and $3,500 for an internship at one of The Claremont Colleges. The two seminars the PTTP scholars take are History and Mission of The Claremont Colleges—which studies the origination, development, transformation, and mission of each of The Claremont Colleges, as well as the unique collaboration of the colleges as a consortium—and Teaching at Liberal Arts Colleges—which prepares students to teach in liberal arts colleges. The course focuses on the liberal arts college student. During their PTTP year, scholars construct two full course portfolios in their discipline, one for a beginning course and the other for an advanced course reflecting their state-of-the-art research interests. The portfolios are provided to prospective mentor faculty members at The Claremont Colleges to arrange for the Scholars' internships and are available in the PFF office to other graduate students.

Results of the CGU FLC PFF Program

The CGU PFF program is in its fourth year. Between thirty and sixty participants have attended each session of the practicum, with over fifty receiving the certificate of completion. Three cohorts of sixteen, eleven, and thirteen have completed the PFF Fellows FLC program, and one cohort of ten has completed the PTTP Scholars FLC program and internship. The 2003–04 FLCs include sixteen PFF fellows and twelve PTTP scholars. Of the PFF fellows, nine have received their PhDs and three their MFAs. (All but one of the remainder are still at CGU.) Several who completed their degrees chose to enter administrative careers (such as director of a service-learning program, head of a private school, or development officer for a museum), but others are in tenure-track or contract faculty positions at academic institutions.

Evaluation of the impact of the FLCs on program elements by the 2002–03 PFF and PTTP cohorts is shown in Table 13.1. The most important impact for participants in both the PFF and PTTP FLCs was on syllabus development. The second highest impact for PFF fellows was on observation of mentor's and others' classes. For PTTP scholars, their teaching projects (portfolios) tied for first place, followed by classroom assessment techniques. (PTTP scholars did not have mentors.) The highest impact on outcomes reported by the PFF fellows was on their understanding of the role of a faculty member, followed by their total effectiveness as a teacher.

Table 13.1. Evaluation of FLC Components by 2002–2003 Cohort Communities, Claremont Graduate University

A. Estimate the impact of the program on you with respect to each of the following program components: "NA" means "does not apply," "1" indicates a very weak impact, and "10" a very strong impact.

FLC Program Components	PFF	PTTP
Syllabus development	8.6 (1)	9.0 (1)
Your teaching project (portfolios)	8.0 (3)	9.0 (1)
Observation of mentor's and others' classes	8.4 (2)	NA
Classroom assessment techniques	7.6 (6)	8.6 (3)
The mentor relationship	8.0 (3)	NA
The colleagueship and learning from the other PFF/PTTP fellows/scholars	7.9 (5)	7.5 (4)
Videotaping	7.2 (7)	6.7 (6)
Seminars	7.1 (8)	8.5 (7)
Retreats and conferences (Lilly West)	6.5 (9)	7.5 (4)

B. In a similar manner, estimate the impact of the program on you with respect to each of the following outcomes: "1" indicates a very weak impact and "10" a very strong impact.

Personal Outcomes	PFF	PTTP
Your understanding of the role of a faculty member	8.6 (1)	8.2 (4)
Your view of teaching as an intellectual pursuit	8.0 (3)	9.0 (1)
Your total effectiveness as a teacher	8.1 (2)	8.2 (4)
Your interest in the teaching process	7.9 (7)	8.7 (2)
Your understanding of and interest in the scholarship of teaching and learning	7.8 (8)	8.7 (2)
Your technical skill as a teacher	8.0 (3)	7.8 (7)
Your awareness of ways to integrate the teaching and research experiences	8.0 (3)	7.4 (10)
Your comfort as a member of the university community	8.0 (3)	7.6 (8)
Your perspective of teaching, learning, and other aspects of higher education beyond the perspectives of your discipline	7.5 (9)	8.1 (6)
Your awareness and understanding of how difference may influence and enhance teaching and learning	7.4 (10)	7.6 (8)
Your research and scholarly interest with respect to your discipline	7.0 (11)	7.0 (11)
Your awareness of ways to integrate the undergraduate and graduate experience	6.3 (12)	5.8 (12)

Notes:

PFF = Preparing Future Faculty program

PTTP = Professional Teaching and Training Program

In each column, the first number is the mean score for that item. The number in parentheses is the ranking of the item.

For PTTP scholars, the highest impact on outcomes was on their view of teaching as an intellectual pursuit, followed by their understanding of and interest in the scholarship of teaching and learning and their interest in the teaching process.

Importance of Community

Although both groups rated colleagueship and learning from the other PFF fellows or PTTP scholars in the middle of the range, their comments when asked "What have you valued most from your participation in the [PFF/PTTP] community?" included several references to the importance of their collegial relationships. A PFF fellow wrote, "I've most valued my professor and classmates—those relationships have become very important to me." And a PTTP scholar cited the "informal nature" of "shared discussion" with other PFF FLC participants. Another indication that the groups valued their community was that eight of the nine PFF fellows and six of the eight PTTP scholars who remained in the area attended the alumni Gathering in December of the following year (the percentages for prior years' attendance at the Gathering also have remained high; all four years of the PFF FLC were represented at the 2003 Gathering). Most returning alumni brought guests or families (there were fourteen children under the age of twelve among the eighty-one guests).

Another indication that community is important to the CGU graduate students is their participation in the CGU topic-based FLCs; over one third of the graduate students in the 2003–04 FLCs on Teaching Women's Studies Courses and on Teaching Research Methods Across the Curriculum are or have been a PFF fellow or a PTTP scholar, and two of the 2002–03 PTTP scholars are FLC cofacilitators of those FLCs. In addition, several students wrote in their course portfolio professional development plans their intention to "be actively involved in faculty learning communities" when they become a faculty member.

References

Lovitts, B. E. *Leaving the Ivory Tower*. Lanham, Md.: Rowman & Littlefield, 2001.

National Study of Postsecondary Faculty. "Table 229: Full-Time Instructional Faculty and Staff in Degree-Granting Institutions, by Instruction Activities and Type and Control of Institution: Fall 1998." Washington, D.C.: National Center for Education Statistics, U.S. Department of Education, 1999.

Preparing Future Faculty National Office. *The Preparing Future Faculty Program*. Washington, D.C.: Association of American Colleges and Universities, n.d.

Rice, R. E., Sorcinelli, M. D., and Austin, A. E. *Heeding New Voices: Academic Careers for a New Generation*. New Pathways: Faculty Careers and Employment for the 21st Century Series, Inquiry no. 7. Washington, D.C.: American Association for Higher Education, 2000.

Richlin, L. "Preparing Future Faculty: Meeting the Need for Teacher-Scholars by Enlarging the View of Scholarship in Ph.D. Programs." Unpublished dissertation, Claremont Graduate University, Claremont, Calif., 1991.

LAURIE RICHLIN is director of the Preparing Future Faculty program and faculty learning communities programs at Claremont Graduate University.

AMY ESSINGTON is a doctoral candidate in American history at Claremont Graduate University and teaches history at California State University, Long Beach.

INDEX

Back Issue/Subscription Order Form

Copy or detach and send to:
Jossey-Bass, A Wiley Company, 989 Market Street, San Francisco CA 94103-1741

Call or fax toll-free: Phone 888-378-2537 6:30AM – 3PM PST; Fax 888-481-2665

Back Issues: Please send me the following issues at $27 each
(Important: please include ISBN number with your order.)

_____

_____

_____

$ _____   Total for single issues

$ _____   SHIPPING CHARGES: SURFACE   Domestic Canadian
                                     First Item $5.00 $6.00
                                     Each Add'l Item $3.00 $1.50
                        For next-day and second-day delivery rates, call the number listed above.

Subscriptions   Please __ start __ renew my subscription to *New Directions for Teaching and Learning* for the year 2__ at the following rate:

U.S.	__ Individual $80	__ Institutional $160
Canada	__ Individual $80	__ Institutional $200
All Others	__ Individual $104	__ Institutional $234
Online Subscription		__ Institutional $145

**For more information about online subscriptions visit
www.interscience.wiley.com**

$ _____   Total single issues and subscriptions (Add appropriate sales tax for your state for single issue orders. No sales tax for U.S. subscriptions. Canadian residents, add GST for subscriptions and single issues.)

__Payment enclosed (U.S. check or money order only)
__VISA __ MC __ AmEx __ #_____ Exp. Date _____

Signature _____ Day Phone _____
__ Bill Me (U.S. institutional orders only. Purchase order required.)

Purchase order # _____
        Federal Tax ID13559302   **GST 89102 8052**

Name _____

Address _____

_____

Phone _____ E-mail _____

For more information about Jossey-Bass, visit our Web site at www.josseybass.com

TL87   Techniques and Strategies for Interpreting Student Evaluations
        Karron G. Lewis
        Focuses on all phases of the student rating process—from data-gathering
        methods to presentation of results. Topics include methods of encouraging
        meaningful evaluations, mid-semester feedback, uses of quality teams and
        focus groups, and creating questions that target individual faculty needs and
        interest.
        ISBN: 0-7879-5789-5

TL86   Scholarship Revisited: Perspectives on the Scholarship of Teaching
        Carolin Kreber
        Presents the outcomes of a Delphi Study conducted by an international
        panel of academics working in faculty evaluation scholarship and
        postsecondary teaching and learning. Identifies the important components of
        scholarship of teaching, defines its characteristics and outcomes, and
        explores its most pressing issues.
        ISBN: 0-7879-5447-0

TL85   Beyond Teaching to Mentoring
        Alice G. Reinarz, Eric R. White
        Offers guidelines to optimizing student learning through classroom activities
        as well as peer, faculty, and professional mentoring. Addresses mentoring
        techniques in technical training, undergraduate business, science, and liberal
        arts studies, health professions, international study, and interdisciplinary
        work.
        ISBN: 0-7879-5617-1

TL84   Principles of Effective Teaching in the Online Classroom
        Renée E. Weiss, Dave S. Knowlton, Bruce W. Speck
        Discusses structuring the online course, utilizing resources from the World
        Wide Web and using other electronic tools and technology to enhance
        classroom efficiency. Addresses challenges unique to the online classroom
        community, including successful communication strategies, performance
        evaluation, academic integrity, and accessibility for disabled students.
        ISBN: 0-7879-5615-5

TL83   Evaluating Teaching in Higher Education: A Vision for the Future
        Katherine E. Ryan
        Analyzes the strengths and weaknesses of current approaches to evaluating
        teaching and recommends practical strategies for improving current
        evaluation methods and developing new ones. Provides an overview of new
        techniques such as peer evaluations, portfolios, and student ratings of
        instructors and technologies.
        ISBN: 0-7879-5448-9

TL82   Teaching to Promote Intellectual and Personal Maturity: Incorporating
        Students' Worldviews and Identities into the Learning Process
        Marcia B. Baxter Magolda
        Explores cognitive and emotional dimensions that influence how individuals
        learn, and describes teaching practices for building on these to help students
        develop intellectually and personally. Examines how students' unique
        understanding of their individual experience, themselves, and the ways
        knowledge is constructed can mediate learning.
        ISBN: 0-7879-5446-2

NEW DIRECTIONS FOR TEACHING AND LEARNING IS NOW AVAILABLE ONLINE AT WILEY INTERSCIENCE

What is Wiley InterScience?

Wiley InterScience is the dynamic online content service from John Wiley & Sons delivering the full text of over 300 leading scientific, technical, medical, and professional journals, plus major reference works, the acclaimed Current Protocols laboratory manuals, and even the full text of select Wiley print books online.

What are some special features of Wiley InterScience?

Wiley Interscience Alerts is a service that delivers table of contents via e-mail for any journal available on Wiley InterScience as soon as a new issue is published online.
EarlyView is Wiley's exclusive service presenting individual articles online as soon as they are ready, even before the release of the compiled print issue. These articles are complete, peer-reviewed, and citable.
CrossRef is the innovative multi-publisher reference linking system enabling readers to move seamlessly from a reference in a journal article to the cited publication, typically located on a different server and published by a different publisher.

How can I access Wiley InterScience?

Visit http://www.interscience.wiley.com.

Guest Users can browse Wiley InterScience for unrestricted access to journal tables of contents and article abstracts, or use the powerful search engine.
Registered Users are provided with a *Personal Home Page* to store and manage customized alerts, searches, and links to favorite journals and articles. Additionally, Registered Users can view free online sample issues and preview selected material from major reference works.
Licensed Customers are entitled to access full-text journal articles in PDF, with select journals also offering full-text HTML.

How do I become an Authorized User?

Authorized Users are individuals authorized by a paying Customer to have access to the journals in Wiley InterScience. For example, a university that subscribes to Wiley journals is considered to be the Customer.
Faculty, staff and students authorized by the university to have access to those journals in Wiley InterScience are Authorized Users. Users should contact their library for information on which Wiley journals they have access to in Wiley InterScience.

ASK YOUR INSTITUTION ABOUT WILEY INTERSCIENCE TODAY!

Printed in the United States
81443LV00003B/93

9 780787 975685